ETERNAL
VICTIM

ETERNAL
VICTOR

ETERNAL VICTIM ETERNAL VICTOR

Donnie McClurkin

Pneuma Life

PUBLISHING

ETERNAL VICTIM ETERNAL VICTOR

Donnie McClurkin

Unless otherwise noted, Scripture quotations are from the King James Version of the Bible. Scripture quotations marked NIV are taken from the New International Version of the Bible. Copyright © 1973, 1978, 1984 International Bible Society. Used by permission of Zondervan Bible Publishers.

Copyright © 2001 Donnie McClurkin
ISBN 1-56229-162-9

Pneuma Life Publishing, Inc.
4451 Parliament Place
Lanham, Maryland 20706
301-577-4052
http://www.pneumalife.com

Printed in the United States of America
    5   7   9   10   8   6   4

CONTENTS

ACKNOWLEDGMENTS

To my mother, father and family.

To the members of the church I pastor, The Perfecting Faith Church, in Long Island, New York; Pastor Marvin L. Winans; Bishop Carlton and Gina Pearson who gave me my first national platform: Azusa; Bishop T. D. and Serita Jakes; Dr. Myles and Ruth Munroe; Pastor Rod and Joni Parsley; and Pastor Benny and Suzanne Hinn.

To all those who prayed for me and to those who read this book, may it be a blessing.

To Derwin and Kimberly Stewart for your patience and perseverance, and for believing in me more than I believed in myself.

INTRODUCTION

How do I begin? This is not an easy task for me by any stretch of the imagination. My idea of what would be my freshman writing was nothing on this wise. After all of the many testimonies concerning my life and my past family ordeals and experiences, I thought that I had finally laid this to rest.

I have been asked for many years to put my testimony to text, yet I've not done so because of the delicacy of the situations, and so that I wouldn't sensationalize and glorify the pain of those experiences, nor cause pain to those involved in these stories.

It was only after starting to write a book of another title that the Holy Spirit changed the direction and led me back to the beginning of matters. Not just to finally bring closure to the entire scenario, but to also lend a face to these types of covert, tumultuous happenings, and show that through the guilt, the pains, the fears, and the loss, there is forgiveness, there is healing, there is restoration of confidence and joy, there is great gain, there is a VICTORIOUS YOU!

What you are reading now is not solely my experience and testimony, but it ultimately involves family members and friends, thus making them vulnerable to the public scrutiny of our intimate events. This is literally the bearing of our souls, and it would be a great disservice to all involved for the reader to take these accounts with a voyeuristic mentality. This is our very life's story.

Remembering and recounting these ordeals resurrects some feelings of hurt and pain that have been long forgotten and calls me to reveal scars of healed wounds, and explain how it happened, how it was endured, and how I, and my family, came out delivered, healed, and victorious. It also gave me great compassion on those who have not healed from their hurts, as well as for those who are still in the midst of their personal hell–especially the children. My goal is to give help and hope to the victim, and encourage and show them how to live as victors.

Victims and victors have one thing in common: SUFFERING! They both encounter conflict, contest, and combat. Each endures hurt, heartache, and hell. Abuse and failure, broken dreams and bouts with identity are commonplace. All of this, they both incur. But it's how they handle these events that classifies whether they are one or the other. But here I go getting ahead of myself. We'll get into this more in-depth as we go along.

So, I pray that through the events of our lives, you will experience the rugged, yet wondrously miraculous road from ETERNAL VICTIM to ETERNAL VICTOR!

1

GENERATIONAL CURSES

I was born on November 9th, 1959 on a Monday evening at around 7:00 p.m. in Lakeside Hospital, Copiague, New York. I was one of ten children (only seven of us are left now) born to the union of my parents.

My father, Donald Sr., was born and raised in Chester, South Carolina. He was one of eight children–four brothers, and four sisters. His father, John McClurkin, was a Baptist pastor of two churches, while his mother, Emma, was the typical southern housewife of that era. She was submissive to her husband in every regard, and was a loving and doting mother to her children and some of her grandchildren.

As was the way of the southern families, when daughters had children out of wedlock, in many cases they were sent south and raised by the grandparents so as to free the young unmarried mothers up to continue trying to rebuild their lives without the stigma of an illegitimate child (or children). My grandmother was that type of a loving woman who cared for our family's children.

On the other hand, when the sons of that era had illegitimate children, they hid and denied the knowledge of them, scarring the children for years until they were older and searched for the truth, themselves. These were children growing up without the love or validation of a father.

My grandfather was a college taught, Baptist theologian who (according to my father) had a great working knowledge of the Bible. Born sometime during the turn of the century in the not too long emancipated South, it was not a common occurrence for a black pastor to be college educated; but "Gramps" was.

A very stern disciplinarian, Gramps was the provider for the family. He wasn't one to play or interact too often with his children. A trait, unfortunately, that my father picked up during his childhood. My grandfather was a man that loved his children and grandchildren; he just didn't know how to verbalize it. Another trait inherited by my dad. Boy, have I learned from this.

Why go back that far? Because in order for you to understand why things happened in my generation, you've got to understand that it got its origin from the generations that preceded it. Time would never allow me to delve as far back into past histories as I would need to go in order to give a detailed analysis of the psychological and sociological ramifications of the dysfunction in... Oh, forget it. I'll simply start where it will be easiest to comprehend.

Dysfunction is not an alien concept to most, if not all, homes in society. Alcoholism, domestic violence, neglect, rejection, substance abuse, sexual abuse, physical abuse, mental, verbal and emotional abuse are relative to everyone, to a certain degree. If not in our homes as adults today, surely in our rearing and upbringing as children in one form or another. So what I incurred is not at all unique. I was simply a child in an unstable home.

My father (like his father before mentioned) was not an emotionally demonstrative man. He was a hard working man—a religiously reared man who was a diligent church-going deacon. He loved his family very much. I believe and know this without a single doubt in my heart and mind. He just didn't know how to express it, openly.

He worked in construction, and built half of our town. I still remember my mother driving us past his work sites and how proud my sisters and I would be seeing him working on that huge backhoe that looked like a dragon. Every now and then, he would bring it home and set it in front of the house. Our greatest joy was to get his permission to go and play on it... pulling levers and making those guttural truck sounds, and feeling that there was nothing better.

During the Christmas holidays, at times he would work more than one job to provide gifts for his many children. There were always presents in abundance, and when we got to a certain age, the presents were replaced with cash—$100.00 each for the eldest three of us, and $50.00 each for the youngest set.

Now, you must understand that during the late 1960's and early 1970's, that was an enormous amount of money, especially for children, and surely it was more than we knew what to do with. We never knew that we were poor. My mother and dad always made sure that we had what we needed. That was never our problem.

Our real problem came from the two providers, themselves. The parents that didn't have the issues of their own past resolved and healed, fought their wars in front of their children, with the children caught in the middle. That's the painful reality: They didn't realize that the children were actually caught in the middle.

My father drank very heavily on weekends and suffered for years with what we called "weekend alcoholism." The memories are still very vivid in my mind. Hearing the arguments at night and getting that tormenting, nervous, fluttering feeling in your stomach as your adrenaline rushed, preparing you for the inevitable violent tussle that would surely pursue. Or, more traumatically, the numbing feeling of coming into the house from school sometimes and seeing furniture toppled and lamps and vases broken into shards and wondering where is your mother and how much physical damage had been done. Seeing the droplets of blood on the floor near the bathroom where your father holds off with a stab wound to his arm. Screaming to the top of your lungs and crying buckets of tears, hoping your emotional tumult would somehow cause them to stop, while jumping in the middle of the floor with your legs and arms flailing like a rag doll, and crying: "Daddy, please take a walk!!! Please, please take a walk!!!" Or to have the police—most repeatedly car 104—tell your father, after the roe, to walk off his anger. Not being able to sleep, worried about what would happen when you heard the front door open upon his return. Caught, helplessly, in the middle! Each parent had their own reasons as to why their war was waged, but what they didn't understand was that the casualty of their war was great; it was their children.

The wounds that were left unhealed in their childhood left deep wounds in us, their children. And if left to run its course, those same wounds and curses would be passed on to the following generation. Each of us (my 5 sisters, my one brother, and myself) carries identifiable scars on our lives from the war of our mother and father.

It would be easy to blame them for the hellish ordeals in our lives, and to accuse them of not caring or thinking about our feelings and how it would affect us. But I've come to realize that it was not their fault.

They were the best parents that they knew how to be in every sense of the word "best". They provided for us, loved us, and sacrificed a whole lifetime for us (even until this day). But the real problem was that they, themselves, were not healed.

My mother was an only child for 20 years. She was reared in a loving home in Harlem, NY, raised by her grandmother, Mary Dinge–affectionately known as "Mumma." Mumma was the product of a home without love. Her mother was a very abusive woman. So, in her young adult life, Mumma tried to fill that loveless void with a series of bad relationships and failed marriages. She had 10 children in her many attempts at relationships, yet, after a series of infant mortalities, only 5 survived.

Her relationship with God changed her entire life, and Mumma raised her family alone, in holiness. She was the first in my mother's lineage to have a relationship with God; and what a relationship she had!

The gifts of the Spirit were in action in her life way before it was widely accepted in the church, in spite of her past. She was a powerfully spiritual woman, called to preach and minister by God. She was originally a member of the Church of God in Christ under the pastorship of the then Elder O. M. Kelly in Harlem, NY.

She was called to preach during an era, not too long passed, that did not believe in, nor accept women clergy. She went to her pastor and informed him of the call of God upon her life to preach, expecting his spiritual guidance on what to do next.

Upon telling him, he replied: "You may have been called to preach, but not in this church!" With that being said, she left and became a member of the Mt. Sinai Holiness Church of America, founded by Bishop Ida Robinson at about the turn of the century. There is where our roots in holiness began.

My mother, Frances, has a quite interesting history that, upon reflection, prompted me to go a little more in-depth than I had originally planned for this book. My mother is 100% proof of God's power to cause you to overcome your past circumstances. Think about it for a moment: She was a by-product of rape. She was fathered by her grandmother's husband. There are still some open wounds that some of our family members carry from this ordeal.

Her grandmother, Mumma, trusted the church members to pray for her, and her family's traumatic situation, believing them to be trust worthy brothers and sisters in Christ. But in turn, they betrayed a broken woman's trust and scandalized her family, brutally. It became a church conversation piece for years to come. Long after my mother was born, the church still circulated the painful ordeal, and their children mocked my mother at five years old continually calling her by the last name of her mother's rapist.

Being raised by Mumma was a bit confusing for my mother. She referred to her birth mother as sister until the age of 16, and for many years she didn't know that Mumma was, in fact, her grandmother, but believed her to be her mother. This was to protect her in an age of society (and the church) that had little compassion for such happenings.

Yet, Mumma and my grandmother instilled and ingrained in my mother something that strengthened her through that otherwise damning experience. They inculcated in my mother throughout her growing up that regardless of how you got here, or what others say about you, or who others say that you are; you are no less than the best! You are more important than you understand, or than others of lesser stuff realize.

These holy matriarchs understood the importance of having a strong, positive identity in Christ, as well as in family. And my mother passed that same strength of identity down to us. Yet, the curse continued.

My mother's adolescent years were during the era of black greatness. She grew up in Harlem, New York during the time that Harlem was "King!" It was the Duke Ellington, Count Basie, Cab Calloway, and Billie Holiday era. Harlem was Black America's Mecca.

My mother was very gifted in singing, and was self-taught in piano. She was offered the opportunity at a young age, to sing professionally in the secular music field. Yet, the convictions that were placed in her from her holy heritage precluded her from accepting.

She sang and played in the church. That's where all of our musical abilities originated–my mother and the church. Our lives were always filled with music and singing. During thunderstorms, all of my sisters and I would rush into my mother's bedroom in fear of the lightning and thunder, and huddle on the bed. In order to take away our fear she would say when it thundered, "Be quiet... God is talking," and she would sing to us.

She would sings songs from her youth in the 1930's, and teach us the words and the three part harmonies at our young ages: Songs like "Small Fry!" and "The Three Little Fishes", and "Narcissus Was a Very Good Looking Boy!"

She would sit at the piano and teach us church songs, and you had to remember your parts. Sitting here typing these memories has me visualizing these events just like it was yesterday and smiling with the warmest of feelings. That's where I get this musical talent.

My first solo was "I Had a Talk with God Last Night!" She would have us sing it in church and stand me on the church table so that I could be seen–as I sang at 4 years old. Memories, like the corners of my mind...

For as long as I can remember, my mother has been a strong willed woman. She told us as children, with a sense of pride–a pride that I now have in her as I tell you on her behalf–how she married my father as a virgin. She shared her growing up experiences with us through the years, and it never ceased to amaze me how interesting her life was.

She communicated well with her children. She was also a hard disciplinarian who raised her children well. She believed in the PROVERBS account. By that, I mean that she applied the rod quite frequently. My siblings and I sit and recount those times and laugh about how mischievous we were, and how funny, in retrospect, those scenarios were. And it may sound a little strange to some of you reading this, but we thank God for the discipline of that day.

In spite of all, we've always been a very close family. We were well watched over as children; and even into my adult years, I didn't know what it was to spend the night over one of my friend's houses. There was a television commercial that would air every night during the 60's and 70's that would ask the question: "It's 10:00! Do you know where your children are?"

That commercial always seemed so strange to me, because in our house, that was such a non-issue. Our parents had to know where we were, seemingly at all times–and we knew exactly when to call it a day and make our way home. The rule was "be home before the street lights come on." You had to be in the yard, not making your way home, before dark.

My God... our greatest fear was to be a little late and to see the silhouetted figure of our father in the distance, waiting in the middle of the street. And our playtime would end early if you heard that whistle that was distinctively our father's.

I sometimes marvel at the similar (almost identical) ordeals that other friends of mine (like my pastor Marvin Winans' family) went through. We sit and listen to each other's stories and laugh so hard sometimes reminiscing our parallel experiences. And, dear Lord, don't let my sisters and brother sit and talk about these past childhood events. We laugh to the point of tearful, sidesplitting exhaustion. Like the "Spare My Life" ordeal...Oh, man... my family must be going crazy reading this part. Don't worry, you guys, I'll save that story for live audiences. :-)

Yet, regardless of the constant protection, the curse continued. On June 6th, 1968, tragedy struck that would alter the affairs of our lives. While playing in the yard on a sunny afternoon in June, with my siblings, I made a neglectful mistake.

I was supposed to be watching my two-year-old baby brother, Thomas, at play, and left him in the un-gated yard to cross the street to retrieve a ball. Unbeknownst to me at the time, he was following me. As my mother was watching out of the living room window, she screamed for me to get the baby. I turned around just in time to see my baby brother struck down by a speeding car in the middle of the street–killed with my mother helplessly watching from the window. My mother got to him just in time to hear his last word: "Mommy!"

We had never experienced this kind of trauma before and my mother was devastated. It was her baby. That was the first funeral my sisters and I had ever attended and I'll never forget it for as long as I live. My mother and father were estranged at the time, and we all had to go and stay at my grandmother's home for a few days so that she could care for my mother.

After seeing that tragic event in front of our home, my mother had to get away. My father went to view the body, and met us there at my grandmother's house. I realize, now, that it must have been much worse for him because he and my mother were separated when it happened.

After a few nights at my Nanna's house, they sent all of us children home to be watched and cared for by our Uncle Clarence. What they had no way of knowing was that this family member was a pedophile. This is the man that scarred my life when I was 8 years old.

It is not necessary to recount the horrid details of this invasion, but that night I was sexually abused and raped by this same uncle, and it caused great hurt and confusion in my life for many years to follow. And there's where the nightmare begins. I realize now that this happened because he, himself, was a broken man. He was unhealed with no one to help him.

In spite of the damage done to and in my life, I understand and forgive him, whole-heartedly. How can I do that? Once YOU are healed, it becomes easy to let things go, and to forgive people, knowing that all things work together for good to them that love the Lord and are the called according to His purpose. Nothing that happened to me could happen to me without the allowance and purpose of God.

So, then, it becomes therapeutic to forgive. I found that forgiving releases you from the stress and anxiety–from the hurt and the hatred. It allows you to finally let go of the bitterness that makes life miserable. Instead, forgiving helps you move on with your real purpose for being, and know that everything that has transpired is destined to work out for your good, if you can somehow see God through it all. After all, we're not the first to go through major dysfunction. Let's look at a biblical example in order to bring out this point. C'mon... the next chapter.

2

IT'S NOT JUST US

*O*ften, we think that our situations are exclusively ours and fail to realize that we are not alone in our ordeals and life's experiences. King Solomon said it best:

> *The thing that hath been, it is that which shall be; and that which is done is that which shall be done: and there is no new thing under the sun. Eccles. 1:9*

It may help for us to realize that all of the great men and women of God before us had some level of great dysfunction, yet they were still mightily used of God. Their dysfunction did not change God's purpose for their lives.

In the words of a great friend of mine, Pastor Rod Parsley, "You can't just read the Bible, you've got to READ the Bible!" So stick with me for a minute as we go through the stories of just a few of these great men. And in reviewing some of their stories, I hope that you can see yourself.

Let's look at a certain family's situation in the book of Genesis. Abraham is known now as the father of faith. But let's take a brief look at this patriarch and deal with some of the less mentioned facts.

Abraham was married to his half-sister and at 74 years old, he had an encounter with God. He believed and followed God's bidding to leave his father's home, and journey to a place that would later be revealed to him as he blindly obeyed God and walked.

Now you've got to understand that Abraham was not raised with a monotheistic belief. His father, Terah, was an idol-maker in Chaldea and worshiped other gods. So, this God that Abraham had never known before, told him that He would make Abraham the father of many nations. The problem was that Abraham's wife Sarah was barren and couldn't have any children. Take note of these situations, for they repeat themselves in Abraham's children's lives.

During their travels, Abraham fathered a lie in order to safeguard himself from marauders who might kill him and take away his wife because of her extreme beauty. He also had sexual relations with his wife's maid, Hagar, to produce a child.

If the truth be told of this father of faith, he found it rather hard to believe that God would do what He said that He would do in the manner that He said that He would do it. So, Abraham messed the whole scenario up by trying to accomplish God's plan through fleshly means.

Yet through it all, he had not aborted the plan of God, and he and Sarah still fulfilled the will of God and brought forth a son, Isaac, at the ripe age of 100 years old. It is quite a spiritual success story. However, they did not realize that the curse was left unbroken and sinful traits would be passed down to the next generation.

Isaac, Abraham's son by his wife, Sarah, was born of faith. He married a young woman by the name of Rebekah. After marriage, he discovered that she, too, was barren and could not have children. As his father Abraham did, so did Isaac. He instructed his wife to tell the same lie just as his father before did with Sarah.

Yet, in spite of his folly, God still blessed Isaac and miraculously opened Rebekah's womb–like his mother's–and Rebekah brought forth twins. She named them Esau and Jacob. And the promise to Abraham continued; yet the curse was still unbroken.

Jacob had an extensive history that we can't get into in this chapter, but let's just get to the point. Jacob carried the lying curse, and became a great deceiver, to the point of stealing his brother Esau's birthright (inheritance) from his dying father, Isaac, by deceiving him into thinking that he was his brother Esau just before Isaac died. He and his mother planned this wicked deception of a blind, aged man during the last moments of his life–on his deathbed. Yet, Jacob was chosen by God to be a mighty nation, Israel.

Jacob had two wives, Leah, and her sister Rachel. Rachel, the wife that he really loved, had the same problem that Jacob's mother and grandmother had. She was barren and could not have children. Jacob had children by his first wife, Leah, and brought forth sons. God opened Rachel's womb, miraculously, and she had two sons, Joseph and Benjamin.

But then Jacob had sexual relations with his first wife Leah's maid (like his grandfather, Abraham) and produced more sons, and then had sexual relations with his wife Rachel's maid, and produced even more sons. With each generation, the curse became more pronounced. Jacob multiplied his father's and grandfather's sin, by far.

Joseph's (Jacob's first son by Rachel) generation was next to carry the curse. Their home was dysfunctional. Jacob showed favoritism to Joseph over all of his other sons, which caused friction amongst the siblings. Joseph's eldest brother slept with his father's concubine, and all of the brothers had a major problem.

Joseph was seemingly destined to carry the curse like his brothers. But instead of following the dysfunctional behavior set by generations past and exemplified in his family's every day living, Joseph broke the curse.

It would have been quite easy for Joseph to resign himself to the pattern set in his home. But instead, he found integrity, honesty, and his identity, and became a great man, despite his family's history.

Joseph was the first to break the generational curse that stained his family's lineage. One father, four sets of children from four different mothers in the same home; acts of jealousy, anger, competition, sexual improprieties, lies, violence, favoritism, vicious plots and betrayal; all of this in the same home.

The home of our biblical patriarchs–those mightily used of God to establish a nation–was dysfunctional. Is that any different from the homes of today? Homes ruined by lies and adultery. Homes in turmoil and jealousy. Homes with one mother, and more than one father of the many children. Sibling rivalries and hatred. You would think that these things would disqualify you. But on the contrary, if you take into account that this is exactly how the homes were of the men and women that were used mightily in the Bible, then that should inspire you to believe that those situations may just be the qualifying factors in God using you and your family in the same way.

These accounts were recorded to help us understand that these men and their families had enormous problems and abusive relationships that scarred them in their day just as badly, and as deeply as we are wounded today. Yet, their faith and obedience to God were the elements that changed the course of their lives, and through the course of time, brought wholeness to them and to their families. But we'll get into the story of Joseph in the following chapters.

All that I want for you to know in this chapter is that it is not uncommon for there to be major dysfunction and obstacles in a life that God has chosen to use for a great purpose. And the hellish ordeals begin at an early age, seemingly before you have any control over them and before you are able to protect, defend or shield yourself from their effects.

From what I read in the Bible and experienced myself firsthand, that's exactly how God likes it because then only He can be credited for salvaging, delivering, restoring, and making you completely whole. So you are not alone, your situation is not unique, but your victorious end is assured if you go through this with these examples in mind.

Joseph had every reason to hate many people. He could have hated his father for the confusing events of his multiple wives and concubines. He could have hated his brothers for their jealousy and hatred of him for no reason except that he received the love of their father, Jacob, that they had longed for all of their lives. He could have hated them for selling him into slavery at such a young age and ruining his relationship with his father, and for robbing him of the years of growing up.

Can you imagine being hated so bitterly by your own family that they actually give you away to strangers and never give it a second thought? How do you forgive that? He could have hated Potiphar's wife for trying to rape him, and then falsely accusing him to her husband because of his non-compliance, thus having this young boy (just broken and devastated by his family's betrayal and separation) thrust for several years into prison for a crime that he never committed.

Joseph had reason to be hardened and calloused toward the world, and we would say that it was justifiable. He could have even hated God. After all, all of this happened because of his integrity with God and man. Why would God allow this to happen to a young boy trying to honor Him? Yet, Joseph realized through all of this that God had a plan for his life, even though he didn't understand what it could possibly be, or why he had to endure such hellish, heartbreaking events from such a young age.

Despite of all of the horror, Joseph was full of integrity in all things–knowing that God was in control. After he successfully suffered through his life's traumas, God elevated him yet again to the position of second in command of all Egypt, and God used him to save the lives of all during the time of great famine.

This man, raised in a totally dysfunctional home, who, statistically, should have been stifled and hindered by the things that he endured, was the one God had chosen to use in order to destroy what was set to destroy him and his family.

Can you see the pattern of your life in these stories of old? And if you have had that kind of hell in your life, just like Abraham, Isaac, Jacob and Joseph, you can also have the glorious results that they had in your life and your family's life. The example is this: You can overcome generations of dysfunction, and through God, and determination have wholeness totally restored, and be mightily used by God regardless of your past encounters.

3

A Seed Is Planted

A major part of my past issues stem from the horrible ordeals that I have encountered. My uncle's molesting and raping me was the beginning of what would be a hard life ahead for me. For years, no...decades, I had to deal with issues that scared and scarred me, deeply.

At the age of 8 years old, a child's mind should be on school and play, on trucks and toys and growing up to be whatever catches his or her fancy for the moment. Those should be the years of innocence, naiveté, and blissful ignorance. But when you thrust a child into adult situations that the child's psyche and mentality has not matured enough to handle, you cause that child to fall into a downward spiral of confusion that is not easily reversed.

At 8 years old, I was hurled into a chasm of confusion by this violation of rape. This "Pandora's Box" was opened in my pre-pubescence, and introduced me to adult sexuality, issues and perversion far beyond my years and definitely beyond my ability to escape without damage.

A seed had been planted... A seed of homosexuality that would be my lot to struggle with for many years to come. Now what I'm about to discuss may not sit too well with some folk, but that can't be helped. I can only tell you what experience has taught me concerning this matter.

Contrary to popular beliefs concerning sexual orientations and proclivities, I was not born with these sexual tendencies. It had nothing to do with some false theory of genetic make-up. It wasn't chromosomal, and had–nor has it in today's society, either–nothing to do with my DNA.

These tendencies that I had and displayed came about because someone touched a little boy. Someone cursed an 8 year old by sexually violating him. Some unhealed, broken man thrust an 8-year-old boy into this whirlwind. Thus my first sexual relationship was with a man. Before I could ever know the purpose or pleasure of a woman, have my first date or even my first kiss, the wound was inflicted and the seed was planted.

Now I know that many people may be expecting me to delve deep into what transpired in my struggle and, in truth, it would probably make much more exciting reading. But the Bible declares that it's a shame to speak of those things that were done in secret. In other words, I can tell you what happened without going into the descriptions and events of such perverse bondage. That would glorify the very thing that I'm writing to reveal and destroy in others.

I received Jesus a year after the rape at the age of 9, but the struggle was just starting. Now, childhood games started to take on a different slant, and rough housing with friends became a little more than adolescent "rites-of-passage" into manhood.

There were feelings and thoughts involved that I knew weren't right. There were compelling desires that made it really difficult to interact with my male best friends, or any males, at all. Attractions started to develop that were seemingly beyond my control at that age.

Can you imagine an eight year old having sexual fantasies about men? Can you imagine the unbelievable thoughts and desires growing in the mind of a child–just a child–that an eight year old is left to fight, alone? How was I supposed to handle this? Who talks to an eight year old about these things?

Now, life began to change and become twisted. Innocence was lost. Male touch or contact activated thoughts and desires that I knew were against God's plan and purpose, but seemed so natural. My imagination became affected and perverse dreams and fantasies of the most gross and unnatural kind developed from seemingly nowhere. I was much too young for such deviant thoughts and images.

Just where did those imaginations and fantasies come from? Such things usually originate from things that are viewed, read, or done. Yet I hadn't viewed, read, or done such perverse things at that age. I realize, now, that I was left uncovered and that there are more forces at play in our lives than just those that are holy and godly. And all of those forces are not working for our good.

There was a war going on to determine my purpose and existence and I didn't even know it. And the war zone was in my mind. My mind was in daily turmoil. I truly mean daily. In school, in church, at home, at play, alone, or with a crowd, reading, watching television, daily. Can you imagine a pre-teen going through such mental and sexual battles?

It seems totally inconceivable, right? But it happens. It happens more often than you may want to realize and it may be your child or loved one going through this secretly and silently. That's why I'm writing this book and especially this chapter. Let me continue...

Watching television was tempting and lust provoking and the sexual innuendoes in the music only made things worse. It was so hard dealing with this struggle in a society that was so submersed in sexual exploitation. To some, this may seem a little extreme and farfetched, but there are those who have experienced—and perhaps are still experiencing—the same type of hell.

My only relief from these things was church. I could go to church and escape the thoughts and feelings, and hear things that intrigued me, greatly. Stories of how the power of God changed other lives. Hearing the older women sit and talk about their growing up in Christ and the miracles that they had witnessed would intrigue me and appeal to my desire to know more about God and His ways.

Stories about meeting some of the great men and women of church history like Bishop C. H. Mason, founder of the Church of God In Christ, and Bishop Ida Robinson, founder of the Mt. Sinai Holiness Churches of America, and one of the first African-American, female bishops. It was another world! It was MY WORLD where I felt at peace and felt like I belonged.

In the daily scheme of things, I was a total misfit. My taboo, secret, homosexual desires made me real shy and reclusive. I didn't play sports with the other boys because I had different feelings that I couldn't explain or understand that made me feel uncomfortable. Not to mention that I was totally inept at anything athletic.

I was born and raised in a sea of women, and didn't know how to adequately interact with men. And because of what was done to me by men, I couldn't relate to men without some type of sexual thoughts and feelings. I couldn't say, "I love you" without some type of sexual desire being attached. This excluded me from most of the normal interactions of my day.

My escape was music. I loved music! I had just started playing the piano at age 11 and I was totally consumed with gospel music. I didn't sing that well, but loved to sing, all the same. I would listen for hours to Andrae Crouch and the Disciples, and fantasize about singing in the group.

I would learn all of the harmonies to all three or four parts of his songs, and every word to the lead and background vocals. Why? Because fantasy convinced me that you never knew when you'd be called to fill in, or in what capacity, so you just had to be ready at all times.

Those were my escape mechanisms from my "issues." Church and Music! Somehow those perversions couldn't bother me there. There was a safe haven there that seemingly removed me from the grasp of the temptation... but only temporarily.

I was 13 when I was sexually molested again. This time it was by my uncle's son, Clarence, Jr. If the seed of homosexual lust and desire was planted with my uncle, it was surely fertilized and deeply rooted with his son's sexual violation of me. I was devastated and told that I couldn't tell or he would do much worse. I believed him and remained silent for years. The only place for me to express myself without total fear was church.

It wasn't long before I discovered that there were many more in the church with these problems that wanted to be free but had to remain silent because this was a taboo issue. They came to church, week after week, looking and yearning for deliverance from this desire. They didn't ask to be this way, nor did they want to stay this way.

They, like myself, were thrust into this before they had a chance or choice in the matter, by someone who left them uncovered, or took advantage of them. I wonder how it would have been if there was someone, anyone, that I could have confided in at a young age, and been mentored and helped by before this seed took root.

I wish the church was that open and ready to deal with this issue and save some young boy or girl before they grow into this and this grows into them. Oh, the lives that we could save and keep from such damage if we, the church, would embrace, love and help those who are struggling with these taboo issues of sexuality. There are a lot of men and women, boys and girls who are involved in this that don't want to be this way.

I discovered that there were VULTURES, also in the church (predatory men that would soon attempt to take advantage of a broken boy and his confusion.) I discovered that in the homosexual lifestyle, when you're young, you are the prey to be hunted. But when you get older, and lose youthfulness, you become the predator.

Every predatory and scavenging creature seeks out the young, weak and wounded. A vulture can smell the sick, infirmed and dying from miles away. Once spotted, they will circle, swoop, and bear down on their prey until they fall and succumb to the constant assault.

And there were brothers who seemingly befriended me under the guise of mentorship, only to reveal their desire and purpose to further the perversion and increase the confusion. My world of security (the church) was invaded when other broken men, in need of healing, made themselves known as predators. Secret lifestyles were revealed, and I was introduced to a deceptive underworld in the church.

Singing on Sundays, after weekend rendezvous was commonplace. Seeing other "Christians" in compromising places, yet faithfully, hypocritically and deceptively at their posts in church as though nothing was wrong was typical.

You became bilingual because this lifestyle had its own "language". You would converse one way with people in general, and a completely different way with the members of your secret inner circle as well as others outside of your circle, yet in the same lifestyle. It was something like radar, no matter where you were, you could detect others with the same lifestyle; as well as be detected.

And being married with children didn't mean anything. Older men perverted younger boys without any consideration of their age or youth, and the same went for the women. All with no thought or concern for the damage that was being perpetuated in those young minds, and the young, in turn, grow older to repeat the same process with the next generation.

Gospel singers, musicians, ministers, pastors, and bishops were hiding their secret lives and living them out in hidden circles. In these cases, there is a plethora to choose from. UNHEALED ministers, singers and those in leadership involved those people who looked up to them with respect and regard. Those brothers and sisters were looking for help from these men and women, but found themselves victims of the unhealed leaders... What a damnable cycle!

Yet in spite of all of this, my love for Christ continued to grow. And in that growth there were those who came to my rescue in order to help with my deliverance. It wasn't the brothers or the men of the church that helped to mold my masculinity. There really weren't enough of them there. If the truth be told, it was the sisters and mothers of the church that became active in the breaking of this curse.

Because it wasn't something that you could speak about openly, or confide in anyone else about, it remained a dormant secret. But the Holy Spirit is a Revealer of secret things, and although these older mothers in the church did not know exactly what it was that I struggled with, the Holy Spirit did reveal to them that there was a struggle.

They would pray with me, talk with me and a few of them–Sister Kitty Braizley in particular–would even teach me how to carry myself like a man. When you wanted to sing soprano, you'd hear them say things like, "Get some bass in your voice!!" or "Men don't sing soprano!" Sister Braizley would teach me how to walk. If you held your hand up in a feminine way, they'd hit your hand and tell you to "Put your hands at your side. Men don't hold their hands like that!"

These small things played a part in the molding and the making of me, but none of these things could have helped me without my desire and determination to be totally and completely made whole.

I, personally, do not believe that there is any such thing as an "unwanted" change. There has to be a sincere desire for change in order for the change to be real and complete. If you are solely changing for others, the change will not be genuine nor will it be lasting. It has to be YOUR desire.

The seed that was planted had to be first destroyed from the root and plucked up. I had to become tired of the torment and seek a genuine exit from the desire. I read in the Scriptures in Ecclesiastes 3, that there is a time to love and also a time to hate, and that struck me as odd because you would never hear anyone preaching about the time to hate.

Any sermons dealing with emotions only addressed the emotions of love, peace, patience, forgiveness, compassion, sadness, etc... but never dealt with why to, what to, who to, and how to hate. I had to learn how to actually hate the thing that was abhorrent to God. EVEN IF IT'S IN ME!!!!

God started to deal with me through that Scripture, and show me what He meant.

1. **Why to hate**—Because He hates the things that are purposed to destroy the ones that He loves–His creation... His children. Also, because it's against His nature, and what He intended for me. He created me to be a man–a whole man–and to love one woman. Anything else is perversion of the male purpose and the female purpose.

2. **What to hate**—I am to hate the thing that is out to destroy me. Whatever it is that's been sent to confuse, delay and deny me of my purpose has got to become my enemy. Mind you, I said WHATEVER not WHOMEVER.

3. **Who to hate**—Now you must be very careful with this one. The church sometimes has a tendency to misdirect their emotions toward what they deem "sin." We turn and condemn the person and hurtfully wield our spiritual hammer, pounding the person instead of the deed. Man, we've damaged and lost so many with our piety and sanctimonious attitudes.

The Bible says in Ephesians 6:12, "For we wrestle not against flesh and blood, but against principalities, against powers, against the rulers of the darkness of this world, against spiritual wickedness in high places." So, our battle is never with a person.

There are some people that we may have to cut off because they bring us back to a place that we are struggling so hard to be freed from; but our hatred is never directed toward that person. It is not a natural enemy that we fight against. For every natural enemy is influenced by a dark, spiritual motivation. We are to look past the persons and see and hate the spirit that's caused these things to happen through the person.

I don't hate the men that sexually abused me in my childhood, nor do I hate the predators that tried to prey on me in my weakness, but what I DO hate is what caused these men to do this. I hate the thing that infected their minds and brought them to the point of damaging a child's life. Be careful how you direct this hatred.

> 4. **How to hate**—You have to make yourself develop a "dislike" for the things that have interrupted your happiness. You have to see wrong for being wrong, and convince yourself that regardless to how you feel, this can never be right. The appetite that has been molded and developed–through years of abuse–for things that are hurtful and harmful for you has got to change, regardless to how comfortable you've become in these situations.

So, I would began to pray, daily, especially when the lust would stir up, "Lord, teach me how to hate! Give me a hatred for what you hate!" I would constantly recite–even until this day–"Every enemy of God, is an enemy of mine!"

Even though the struggle continued, I found that the more I immersed myself in the study of the Scriptures and used those Scriptures during my temptation, the more I began to win the battle.

> *Wherewithal shall a young man cleanse his way? by taking heed thereto according to thy word. With my whole heart have I sought thee: O let me not wander from thy commandments. Thy word have I hid in mine heart, that I might not sin against thee. Psalm 119:9-11*

I found out that you can know the Scriptures—or whatever help mechanisms you have available—and never use them and fail in your struggle. But when you use them in the midst of your temptation, they give you the strength to overcome the struggle.

I don't want you to think that it is just that simple. There are many more things that need to be done to break the curse of homosexuality; but that's another book. These are just some of the things that brought me to total deliverance. The seed was killed from its root, plucked up and now there is a seed of righteousness that's incorruptible.

Luke 8:11 states that the Word of God is that incorruptible seed. It is of the utmost importance that the seed (*sperma*) of His Word be planted in your heart (mind) in order for you to maintain deliverance. I use this analogy: When a woman is impregnated, a seed is planted in her womb and once that seed takes root in the egg, it stops the natural cycle and thus the baby begins to grow.

It's the same with the Word of God. When the seed is planted into the heart of the man, if used correctly, it will stop the natural cycle of sin; that Word will multiply and grow in that man. That seed will bring forth fruit and the fruit will remain.

Now there may be some that will read this and resent some of the statements made about homosexuality. I understand. For some, there is no desire to change this lifestyle because they believe that is who they are and who they were meant to be.

There are those who believe that God made them that way and they are happy in their sexuality. Then this is not for you. But please understand that there are countless numbers of people that are not happy in this lifestyle and with these desires and they want to be delivered and freed from it. There are those who were thrust into homosexuality by neglect, abuse and molestation and want, most desperately, to live a normal life and one day have a happy home and family.

For them, I write this without apology, knowing that I've been through this and experienced God and His power to change my lifestyle. I believed that I was meant to be a whole man, made for one woman and God brought it all about. What you've just read is what I went through, what I still have to deal with in some sense and how I was delivered (and let it be known that I AM DELIVERED) and that's what I recommend for you.

My sister Olivia (with mask), Donnie,
Dad, my sister Marlene, Aunt Ardel. 1960

Donny at age 7

Uncle Clarence, the man that
raped me when I was 8 years old

My 2 year old brother Thomas,
about two weeks before his death

Aunt Gladys, Mother, Aunt Florine, little Thomas

Front Row: My cousin Clarence, Jr. and our dog Chipper
(As had his father, Clarence, Jr. raped me when I was 13)
Second row: Marlene, Mother holding Thomas, Olivia
Back row: My cousin Linda, my sisters Cheri and Andrea,
Donnie

This picture was taken in 1968, days before Thomas died

**Andrea at one year, Cheri
at age 2, Donnie at age 3$^{1/2}$**

My youngest sister Tonya (8 months old)

Andrea at one year old

My sisters Marlene (18 months old)
and Olivia (7 months old)

Cheri, Donnie, Andrea, Olivia (standing). 1972

Olivia at age 12, Donnie at age 10, Marlene at age 13

4

IT WON'T WORK

*I*t has been found, in many cases, that when we've been victimized, we become emotionally affected in some ways and in areas of our lives that, without the proper counsel and care, cripple us.

Victims often suffer from poor "self-image" issues—low or no self worth or esteem, self-hatred and insecurities. In many cases, victims are easily intimidated and fearful, many times needing validation and approval from others to feel accepted. To not be validated and approved by the ones that we view as authorities or superior to us, or anyone for that matter, is considered painful rejection. The rejection causes us to try harder to fit in and gain acceptance. But, in reality, it only worsens the problem, and continues the abuse cycle.

Until we allow ourselves to heal, we will carry a latent anger within toward others, anger with ourselves and a SELF-HATRED. Why? Because we've allowed our self-image to be molded, affected—and more accurately, infected—by the people, words and situations that caused this pain and damage in our lives.

You know, we promised that we'd be stronger and stand up for ourselves. We vowed that we wouldn't let anyone else run over us, yet we buckled again. Laughing at things that aren't funny, even when those things are about you, just to try to fit in. Totally insecure. For the most part, those suffering with these insecurities haven't had anyone to give them a strong sense of their identity at an early age.

You see, it's hard to break old, set patterns that have grown in us with every year of our existence. What didn't happen when we were young–stability in the home, affirming parents, strong fathers to foster strong men, caring mothers to breed secure, feminine daughters, and loving interaction between husband and wife–cannot easily be revisited and re-done once we are older. It really is hard to teach an old dog new tricks. Hard, but not impossible.

For with God nothing shall be impossible. Luke 1:37

People say, "Sticks and stones may break your bones, but words can never hurt you." That is the biggest lie that anyone can ever tell because it's easier to heal from the wounds of sticks and stones that leave temporary marks and pain, than from the words that cut like a knife and take years to overcome–if they're overcome at all. If you hit me in the head with a brick, I may need some stitches and suffer a possible concussion or even a fractured skull that will heal in a little while, but if I'm hit in the heart with evil spoken words, neglect, abuse or rejection, how do I heal from that?

Those words, spoken in anger to children by respected adults, cut like a razor into their psyche and affect their self-image in such a terrible way. Words like "You make me sick!" "You're just like your father!" "Get out of my face!" "You can never do anything right!" "You're worthless!" Those words cause serious psychological damage. Those words and those opinions somehow seem to take on life and affect the lives of those that these words were hurled at.

These are words that the enemy purposed to destroy future potential and to stifle greatness. These are words that shatter dreams and spoil futures. But I stand to serve you notice, that although you've been hurt, wounded, stymied and stifled in your past by situations, words, and people, you are NOT beyond repair. Yes, I do mean TOTAL, COMPLETE repair.

Understand this, foremost. Every negative thing that was said about you in the past is of no consequence! Regardless of all of your mistakes and faults, you are not a failure! You need to take a few moments from reading this book and declare this out loud right now "I am not a FAILURE!"

People have a tendency to judge others by their past, thus condemning them to their past, seemingly without reprieve. We judge others in regard to their sin and their mistakes. People seem to always notice the falls. But they don't stick around long enough to witness the person getting back up after the fall.

But what I always say is don't judge me by my past. What was in my past is just that... in the past. I've grown in so many ways and changed with every passing experience.

*Rejoice not against me, O mine enemy: **when** I fall, I shall arise; when I sit in darkness, the LORD shall be a light unto me. Micah 7:8*

What is very interesting about this is the word WHEN in that verse. It didn't say IF, but WHEN. In other words, in our lifetime, it is a sure guarantee that we will mess up, fail, and fall in one manner or another. It's inevitable! But the fall is not the focus in this Scripture; it's the rising.

Why is it that religious people pretend as though these things do not happen? Why is it that there is such a lack of tolerance? We ALL have sinned and fallen short of that perfect mark, so who can condemn another? So, we find that it's not just "Satan" that we have coming against us, but it's also the hypocritical "religious" church zealots. But despite all of the opposition from whatever angle, we're still here.

What the enemy purposed and used to try to destroy you failed because, to his great disappointment, you're still here. His purpose was not just to cause you hurt and leave you emotionally and psychologically wounded. He didn't just want to make your childhood and life a living, dysfunctional hell, as horrible as it might have been. That was not his purpose. His purpose, the Bible says, is to "steal, kill and destroy"; if you are still alive, then by that reason alone, you stand in direct defiance of the enemy's purpose.

Everyday you wake up, no matter what hell you have been through or happen to be going through NOW, serves as living proof that the enemy has failed at his task; he didn't then, nor does he now, have the power to do what he said that he would. These are things that he doesn't want you to know, but just by reason of your existence now, just by sitting here reading this book, proves that neither the devil, nor people, could accomplish what they wanted to do in your life.

What you have been through was purposed to kill you. You were not supposed to be able to walk away intact. Many people have lost their minds and their lives over less than what you've been through. So why are you still here? Because there is a purpose for your life, far greater than any plot or plan of people or the devil himself to destroy you. YOU HAVE TO LISTEN TO LIFE!

You can look at your situation—no matter how awful your past or present—and tell the devil, "You should have killed me when you had the chance, but it's too late now. You don't have that kind of power!" Tell yourself, tell your family, your friends AND your enemies, "It won't work!" What others have said you cannot do because of what they believe to be your lack of qualifications cannot be allowed to cancel what God purposed for you to do and to be.

Let them know that what they think about you will not stop you; IT WON'T WORK! The truth is what they think about you doesn't matter, at all. And if it's a choice between people validating you and your purpose being fulfilled, kiss the people goodbye!! Prove them wrong by fulfilling your purpose. LISTEN TO LIFE!

Finally declare, "I won't be a victim to poverty. I won't be a victim to my past. I won't let anybody's opinion of me hold me hostage any longer, nor will I be held hostage to religious dogma that is not based on Scripture, but based on control."

You've allowed yourself to be beaten by the thoughts and words of others; you've even beaten yourself by believing your own insecurities, but NO MORE! Fling everyone's negative opinions back in their faces and live up to your fullest potential. Have a change of heart, change of mind and even change of speech and declare that failure is not an option! "I WILL LISTEN TO LIFE!"

Proclaim victory over those past ordeals. When the enemy attacks your mind, life, finances, family, job, relationship... whatever... remember and declare, "IT WON'T WORK!"

5

YOU WERE BORN FOR THIS

*I*f, indeed, we believe in providence, and that nothing happens by chance or coincidence; and if we believe that there is a God and that He is really in control of our entire lives, then we have to believe that we were purposed and empowered to go through and endure all of our life's encounters. NOTHING happens without a purpose.

> *Pilate therefore said unto him, Art thou a king then? Jesus answered, Thou sayest that I am a king. To this end was I born, and for this cause came I into the world, that I should bear witness unto the truth. Every one that is of the truth heareth my voice. Pilate saith unto him, What is truth? And when he had said this, he went out again unto the Jews, and saith unto them, I find in him no fault at all. But ye have a custom, that I should release unto you one at the passover: will ye therefore that I release unto you the King of the Jews? Then cried they all again, saying, Not this man, but Barabbas. Now Barabbas was a robber. John 18:37-40*

In John 18, Jesus was brought before Pontius Pilate. Pilate asks his accusers, "What accusation do you bring against this man?" After they had rendered their false accusations, Pilate returns to Jesus and tells Him that His own people have delivered Him up to be put to death. HIS OWN PEOPLE! Jesus then states, "To this end was I born, and for this cause came I into the world." Now there is something significant about this saying. What is Jesus saying that He came into this world to do?

I submit to you that He, in essence, is saying that He came to be rejected and belittled and beaten–that He came to endure false accusations. He came to be hurt, wounded, bruised and ultimately, He was born to die. So, His purpose was to be born into this world to suffer and die for us all and thus bring salvation to all who will believe on Him.

> Forasmuch then as Christ hath suffered for us in the flesh, arm yourselves likewise with the same mind: for he that hath suffered in the flesh hath ceased from sin; 1 Peter 4:1

We are instructed in the Bible to arm ourselves to do likewise. What does that mean? That means as Christ had to suffer, and was born to suffer, so also are we.

> Man that is born of a woman is of few days, and full of trouble. Job 14:1

Everyone is born to endure their own hells and struggles. EVERYONE! But what you need to know is that the personal hell and struggle that you were born into has a specific purpose. The purpose is not to destroy you, although it feels like it sometimes, but the purpose is for you to overcome them. Not only to endure them, but to conquer and OVER-

COME THEM! Why? So that you can help others that are in similar situations.

> *Looking unto Jesus the author and finisher of our faith; who for the joy that was set before him endured the cross, despising the shame, and is set down at the right hand of the throne of God. Hebrews 12:2*

Oh! If we could only learn from this Scripture and realize that there is joy after our suffering. What was the joy that was set before Jesus that would make it worth His enduring the suffering on the cross, and disregarding the shame and humiliation? It was the joy of seeing others made whole and set free through the things that He suffered for their benefit.

This came by way of His resurrection from the dead. He suffered and died, but after His death came His resurrection. His resurrection gave hope to all those who are laden with sin and are in need of deliverance. So to, we seemingly suffered death through the ordeals of our past because of the horrendous things that we've endured. Yet, after all these crushing ordeals, there is a resurrection for us—a rising from the rubble and a healing from the hurts and pains that will bring help to others in need once they see that we've successfully overcome.

Our painful experiences from our past can serve in helping others that are going through like situations in this present time. Our hurt and healing—and our pain and progress —have actually been purposed to help and heal someone else. But it takes a lot of understanding of purpose to realize this. Jesus set the example. He let us know that He was born to go through this.

I have to go back to Joseph, again. In Genesis 37, Joseph was born to be hated and to suffer at the hands of his own brothers. He was born to be sold in slavery by his own flesh and blood to the wandering Ishmaelites for 20 pieces of silver and brought to Egypt. He was born to be torn from the fabric of his family and home.

He was born to be humbled to the status of a servant to an Egyptian officer named Potiphar—after having lived in a wealthy home with a wealthy family. He was born to be falsely accused of sexual advances and thrown into prison by Potiphar's wife. He was born to be forgotten there for 2 years, while others that he ministered to were released. All of this happened to Joseph simply because he believed God had a great purpose for him.

Now some would say, "How can this be fair? Why would this happen to someone who had such faith in God?" And Joseph might have believed and said the same if he judged who he was by his situations, but the story is not over and neither is yours.

Because Joseph continued to believe, he found that he was also born to be delivered from the prison to the palace. He was born to be brought before Pharaoh himself. He was born to deliver Egypt, and the world as they knew it, from the famine. He was born to be the mouthpiece of God and bring salvation to the people, and to be reunited with his brothers and father after years of separation and his father believing him to be dead.

He was born to forgive them and LOVINGLY thank them for what they did. He was born to be made the second greatest man in all of Egypt. He was born for all of this!

In 1 Samuel 16, a little boy named David, who was born to be king, was also born to be overlooked and discounted by his father. In chapter 17, he was looked down upon by his own brothers, but he was also born to be used by God; and for the sake of the entire nation of Israel, he was born to kill a giant by the name of Goliath. But that's not the end of his suffering. David was also born to be hated by the reigning king because of his victories. He was born to have spears thrown at him by this King Saul, and born to run and hide in caves and suffer humiliation at the hand of the king he vowed to serve.

All of this, just because God had a purpose for him. And now, let's see the real reason why David was born. He was born to be a mighty warrior that would lead his country into many victories. He was born to be a great leader of the armies. He was born to be the most noted king of all Israel. He was born to be in the lineage by which Jesus was to come. He was born for this.

Through these stories, I want for you to realize that no matter what your history or no matter what your dysfunction, you were born to be the head, and not the tail. Even though you may have lost many battles in the past, that doesn't negate the fact that you were born to be always triumphant. No matter how low you are and may feel, you were born to be above and not beneath. You were born to be MORE than a conqueror.

No matter how bleak things have been and possibly still are, you were born to be victorious! You may have been born into poverty, but you were not born to stay impoverished. You were born for prosperity. You may have been born into a hell-

71

ish home filled with domestic troubles, but you were not born to repeat it nor remain scarred from it. You were born to live life, much fuller and abundantly.

Don't be fooled, you can take this. You've made it this far, you can make it the rest of the way. It may hurt, but it will not overcome you because, YOU WERE BORN FOR THIS!

6

GET OVER IT

*S*ympathy, to an eternal victim, is like a drug to which they develop an addiction. The more they get, the more they want. Although I sympathize with people and their plights, there has to be a limit. I find it rather difficult to continue to listen to people's sob stories who refuse help, and are comfortable with just rehearsing their saga to as many as will listen, and resisting any efforts toward real change.

You can only cry but so much before people get tired. Because believe it or not, everybody has their own soap operas that they are going through, and most folk just don't have the time to sit back and accommodate "pity" addicts.

I am not being harsh and uncaring, nor am I being uncompassionate. I understand hurt and I understand people's dilemmas and painful past, but you can't live in that past. And you surely can't make me live in it along with you.

It's time to move on and get back into life—real life. Because, believe it or not, there is a life beyond your pain and there is a life beyond your past.

Let me put this as nicely and as sensitively as I possibly can: GET OVER IT!!

Now, I know that it's not easy, by any stretch of the imagination, to break free of the mental images, words and scars that come from your past. But just because it's not easy doesn't mean that you resign yourself to stay there. Yes, it's going to take work, and you will have to make a conscious effort. To be truthful, it's going to be a long, hard journey, but it's one that you need to take in order to be free... mind, soul and spirit.

> I beseech you therefore, brethren, by the mercies of God, that ye present your bodies a living sacrifice, holy, acceptable unto God, which is your reasonable service. Romans 12:1

> And be renewed in the spirit of your mind; Ephes. 4:23

The mind is the seat of your emotions and it is where most of the damage is done. If you can find, through faith and/or counseling, how to relieve yourself of the mental burdens, you will be able to cope, no matter what the situation. It's quite possible for the mind to be free even in the middle of total turmoil.

There are many men and women that are incarcerated in our penile facilities who, although jailed and bound, refuse to be so in their minds. Thus, they can cope with the time that they have to spend there, knowing that although their bodies may be in prison, there souls can be free as a bird; that makes their spirit indomitable. So should we all be.

Beloved, I wish above all things that thou mayest prosper and be in health, even as thy soul prospereth. 3 John 1:2

The soul and the mind are really synonymous, so when the Bible says, "even as thy soul prospereth," it denotes mental and emotional wholeness. How can you prosper in a perpetual state of depression? How can you be in health when your mind and emotions are in constant turmoil?

Your body reacts to the ordeals of your mind. So mental health and wholeness is just as important as physical health and wholeness, because they are directly linked together. Your mental state causes physical ailments and maladies. Constant stress and anxiety can cause ulcers, migraine headaches, high blood pressure, heart conditions, faintings, nervous breakdowns... and the list goes on and on. All of these ailments stem from the troubled mind or "soul". In the words of the United Negro College Fund, "A mind is a terrible thing to waste."

There are people that I know, personally, who live in a perpetual state of mental hell and depression and actually refuse to move from their point of abuse, regardless to how long ago it was. I know a woman who suffered a tragedy over six decades ago and now, as an octogenarian, still acts like the ordeal just happened whenever the situation is mentioned. It was over sixty years ago, and she's still angry, still hurt, still on the defensive, and still crying.

It's like she's living in her own prison. She didn't want to have anything to do with any of her siblings. It's so bad that she didn't even attend the funeral of her only brother and hasn't spoken in years to her only remaining sibling. There are many others like her.

Now, I'm not a psychologist, but I do know that there is a way to break free from that type of painful prison, and it starts in the mind.

Thou wilt keep him in perfect peace, whose mind is stayed on thee: because he trusteth in thee. Isaiah 26:3

Finally, brethren, whatsoever things are true, whatsoever things are honest, whatsoever things are just, whatsoever things are pure, whatsoever things are lovely, whatsoever things are of good report; if there be any virtue, and if there be any praise, think on these things. Philip. 4

As I said previously, this takes a conscious effort on the part of the one who is trying to change. You've got to make yourself relinquish the abusive and painful thoughts in exchange for thoughts that are good, and pure, and true, and just, and lovely, and of good report, and are virtuous, and are praiseworthy.

Just like it's quite impossible for you to build a healthy body without some type of action, motion, or exercise, the same applies to mental health and wholeness. You need a daily mental workout of sorts. Exercise your mind with good thoughts, kind words, lovely images and things that are pleasant to remember. Make yourself do this. Force yourself to think on those things that are thought worthy. Train your mind to develop a healthy habit of happy thinking and let go of the painful past, day by day.

It would be easy for me to hold on to memories of the abuse of my family's past, and remember the painful ordeals and events that happened to me. I could remember and hold anger against the people that have wounded me in my days gone by. But I choose to release them of all culpability and to let them "off the hook," because life has got to keep moving on.

I have got to live a life of real joy. I have got to live a life of happiness and I cannot be weighed down by the memories of days gone by that I can't change–memories of days that will bring me down lower. It's time to get up and move on out.

> Brethren, I count not myself to have apprehended: but this one thing I do, forgetting those things which are behind, and reaching forth unto those things which are before, Philip. 3:13

I wrote a song that I guess I will release on my next CD and the words are quite touching. When God gave this song to me–yes, God does sing–He showed me MYSELF and spoke these words of closure:

> *I know that you've been hurt and how you've been abused.*
> *Yes, I know... But let's move on from here.*
> *I know your heart's been broken and how you're feeling used.*
> *Yes, I know... But let's move on from here.*
> *Ohhhh... You've cried so many tears.*
> *You've lived inside your fears.*
> *But it's another day, So, I say...*
> *Take My hand, and let's move on from here.*
> *You can't live in the past.*
> *You can't remain in the pain.*
> *It's a new day... and time for letting go.*
> *You're not there anymore. Take My hand, close the door.*
> *Ohhhh... Take my hand and let's move on from here.*

You have to let go and stop lamenting about the things of the past. You have to find a way, through faith or counseling, to forgive the ones that did you evil. You have to forgive the abusers and misusers. You have to get over the "victim'" mentality before it causes you any more damage. You have got to get over the "licking of your wounds."

One way or another, you have to leave those things in the past and start reaching to a new life. Press into your future with the confidence that it will be nothing like your past. You must reach a place of happiness and find the joy in living. Let all your misery and tormenting memories die here, and walk as the Bible says, "in the newness of life." That's where you belong.

7

TRY AGAIN

*I*f you're not afraid of failure, you can ultimately accomplish anything. "If, at first, you fail your deed, try again 'til you succeed!" What an idealistically inspiring adage.

Failure only allows you another chance to assess what you've done wrong and another opportunity to troubleshoot it until you perfect it. So, failed attempts at a goal only serve as stepping-stones to ultimate success.

The problem that most "victims" have is that they judge themselves by their failures and not by their divine and God-given ability to achieve, to attain, to be successful in whatever they have the capability of doing–and BEING!

They really don't believe themselves to have the power to accomplish anything worthwhile or life changing. While others can see the potential in them, they can't accept their own greatness because they can only see and judge themselves by their past failures.

For those who have been victimized, to try and then fail means to stop trying altogether or risk facing humiliation and rejection. They have allowed their victimization to stifle their progress. They are already victims of low self-esteem and they cannot accomplish the things they want to because of an inner nagging which convinces them that they are doomed to mess up. In their fear, they fail to realize that success is gained through a series of trials, errors and failures, as well as tenacity and determination to keep plugging away until the goal is met.

Tenacity, determination, faith and hope must be our only resolve for setbacks and failure. Remember that failure in life is never a red light, which means to stop. But it's a yellow light, which means proceed with caution. This caution is not fear of failing again, but caution is using what you have learned from your experience of failure as new knowledge and wisdom to achieve and not fail on the next attempt or many subsequent attempts.

Let's take a look at Abraham Lincoln's failures and successes:

YEAR	FAILURES or SETBACKS	SUCCESSES
1832	Lost job Defeated for state legislature	Elected company captain of Illinois militia in Black Hawk War
1833	Failed in business	Appointed postmaster of New Salem, Illinois Appointed deputy surveyor of Sangamon County
1834		Elected to Illinois state legislature
1835	Sweetheart died	

YEAR	FAILURES or SETBACKS	SUCCESSES
1836	Had a nervous breakdown	Re-elected to Illinois state legislature (running first in his district) Received license to practice law in Illinois state courts
1837		Led Whig delegation in moving Illinois state capital from Vandalia to Springfield Became law partner of John T. Stuart
1838	Defeated for Speaker	Nominated for Illinois House Speaker by Whig caucus Re-elected to Illinois House (running first in his district) Served as Whig floor leader
1839		Chosen presidential elector by first Whig convention Admitted to practice law in U.S. Circuit Court
1840		Argues first case before Illinois Supreme Court Re-elected to Illinois state legislature
1841		Established new law practice with Stephen T. Logan
1842		Admitted to practice law in U.S. District Court
1843	Defeated for nomination for Congress	

YEAR	FAILURES or SETBACKS	SUCCESSES
1844		Established own law practice with William H. Herndon as junior partner
1846		Elected to Congress
1848	Lost renomination	(Chose not to run for Congress, abiding by rule of rotation among Whigs)
1849	Rejected for land officer	Admitted to practice law in U.S. Supreme Court Declined appointment as secretary and then as governor of Oregon Territory
1854	Defeated for U.S. Senate	Elected to Illinois state legislature (but declined seat to run for U.S. Senate)
1856	Defeated for nomination for Vice President	
1858	Again defeated for U.S. Senate	
1860		Elected President

No matter how many times you lose an election, or how limited your education is, if your tenacity and your determination are strong, you will jump over every hurdle. You may hit the hurdle a few times, stumble and even fall, but don't stop the race. Keep moving.

All too often, victims become paralyzed with the first hurdle that falls, because they consider themselves losers even before the race is underway. They become obsessed with how people view them, and what people will say about them. It stops them. It hinders them. It paralyzes them.

In order to overcome an obstacle, even one laden within, you first need to acknowledge that the problem exists. Merely having a five-point or five-step program is not going to help those that are already blocked in their mind. You see, the enemy's battle is waged within. It is in one's mind, where they suffer the agony of defeat, day in and day out.

What good will it do for me to elaborate on some twelve-step, ten-step, or five-step program on how to get out of your funk or how to overcome your insecurities when your mind is imprisoned? First, admit that there is a problem. Acknowledge your fear of failure and dread of doing challenging things. Stop convincing yourself that you cannot do things or must depend on others because you think that they are better than you. If you have low self-esteem, deal with that. You need to believe that you truly are capable of producing grand things, alone.

If you persist in having negative thoughts about yourself, you will never accomplish any achievements. Deal with your fear, my friend. Fear will only paralyze, hinder, and stop you from progressing to some of the greatest successes of lif and maybe that this world has ever seen.

That may sound grandiose, perhaps even a bit extreme, but that's the way most major players in the world started. They dared to dream big dreams and do what they had to do in order to accomplish them. They too had to overcome their fears, their insecurities, and their idiosyncratic ways and habits. They had to overcome ridicule and the insecurities of not being pretty enough, or smart enough, or rich enough. They refused to mull over not being educated at the best schools, or growing up in the wrong household. They reached the point where they said, "Enough is enough. I can do this."

When people laughed at them, mocked them, and counted them unworthy, they did not waver from their course. The goal was already set. Just like Bill Gates, Oprah Winfrey, Maya Angelou, and Abraham Lincoln, something motivated them even though there were many reasons they could have sat back and said, "I can't do this. I am not qualified."

They threw off their fears, showed some tenacity, and developed a strong determination to overcome the obstacles in their lives. Surely, there were situations that could have caused them to be just another loser with a great dream, unable to ever make that dream manifest. But, they did not buckle. They did not quit. They grabbed a hold of their dream and said, "It's either do or die trying."

Every victor had levels of fear that they had to overcome. They had the choice of remaining a victim, never doing anything worthwhile, barely making it, keeping a menial job, and being the support for everyone else's dream. Instead, with each accomplishment, they went higher. They knew that if they could achieve one goal, then they could achieve another.

Every person that has ever accomplished anything has a testimony. A victim is blind to the fact that every victor had their own fair share of fears and failures to overcome. The difference between the victor and the victim is that the victor did not stop at the point of failure–he overcame it.

It is essential that the victim deal with his fears. Failure is not the end of a situation. Fight! Force yourself to overcome. It will not be easy, especially alone. But guess what? If you do not have support systems, then you will just have to do it by yourself. Get to the point where your dysfunction becomes uncomfortable.

Aren't you tired of seeing life pass you by? Aren't you tired of erecting ridiculous mountains of excuses? What happened to your dreams? Don't you know that there is a way of making your dream your reality? It just takes boldness. You will have to cast aside your fears and grab a hold of that thing that seems like it is more than you can chew. Brace yourself now for the fact that you will encounter opposition. On your road to recovery, there will undoubtedly be pain, hard knocks, loss, and even failure; but realize that it is just the pavement to your place of victory!

Prepare yourself now to go through it. Endure! Nobody achieves any measure of success without struggle and without a fight. In order to reach your desired end, you have to be willing to scrape your knees a few times, sweat a bit, and force yourself out every comfort zone you have. Get to the next level!

Success means that you have got to have an excellent spirit. Excellent does not mean perfect or the greatest apex or the greatest level. When you have a spirit of excellence, complacency and mediocrity become overwhelmingly unbearable for you. You find it nearly impossible to rest on your laurels because you sense that there are even greater things to do. Excellence always challenges you to do more.

You simply cannot be bound or governed by fear and still operate in excellence. You cannot be paralyzed, stifled, and stymied by your past and still have excellence. When nothing short of excellence is your target, you begin to force yourself to move on. From the bottom of the heap, you can still hear excellence crying for you to get up.

You may have been a welfare abuser or drug abuser. You may live in a rough neighborhood or lack education, yet you can still hear excellence telling you to move. You may have nothing in your past to refer to except failure, but that's okay. All you really need, my friend, is your determination. You see, your circumstances pale in comparison to what is in store for you, if you just don't give up.

Stop saying you are tired of where you are and get up and do something about it. Ready yourself to do great things. You do not need to start great in order to finish great. Your present circumstances should never sway you from treading along your road to success.

What's your game plan? If you did not finish school, start taking classes for a GED. Once you achieve that, don't stop. Go to college. You see, once you receive your GED, you will have established a track record. When doubt or fear arises, you will be able to remember that you got up from the rubble before, and you can certainly do it again. Even if it takes 8 years to finish a 2-year course, do it.

Each success and failure, victory and defeat, should only serve to get you to your next level. Learn from your mistakes. Revel in your successes and victories for a moment, and then move on to your next triumph. You have the power to determine your destiny and scorecard, but you have to get to the point of being uncomfortable where you are.

I am pastor of Perfecting Faith Church in Long Island, New York. At my former church, Perfecting Church in Detroit, Michigan, they welcome people that are down and out. We don't look down on them because they are on welfare or homeless. We gladly tell those people to come on in, and we embrace them like they are the richest people in the world. But, we also tell them that we will not allow them to stay down and out or remain in a place where they can be helped, but refuse to accept it.

We have tutoring classes for students, both young and old. We have transitional houses for battered women, outreaches for drug addicts, and a whole slew of other services. You see, it does not matter how they came to church. What matters most is what they do after they come. If the person is not ready to fight and get out of their dysfunctional comfort zone, then there is nothing anyone can do to help them. They have to realize where they are and what they are dealing with and have a real desire to change.

Inch-by-inch and step-by-step, move. Don't stop. When it seems as if you have hit a brick wall, don't quit. Walk around it, tunnel through it, climb over it, but don't stop just because the wall exists. Keep moving. That is the difference between being a victim and being a victor. Both of them deal with the same struggles. Victors have to deal with the same fears that cause victims to fall. A victor does not have anything extra, except determination. They refuse to give in to failure—not refuse to fail—but refuse to give in to that failure.

91

Now, let me clarify something, being rich does not make you an automatic victor. It may make it easier for you in some ways, but it does not exempt you from whatever fears and insecurities you face. Also, just because you may not have grown up in a dysfunctional home does not make you an automatic victor either. You may function in society with a greater level of ease, but there are still other struggles that challenge you.

Have you ever given any consideration to the problems the royal families of England and Monaco face? They are affluent and surrounded by palatial grandeur. They have beauty, brains, and bucks, but they also have their share of struggles. They too become victims of their fears. So, you see, no one is exempt from having to overcome obstacles–not you, not I, not even someone like Princess Di.

Do you know that the day that the challenge stops is the day that you slide back into total dysfunction? The day that there are no more struggles, life is no longer worth living. Consider a newborn baby: When a baby comes out of the womb and does not start breathing on its own, it is stillborn. But after the first breath, we proudly announce that it is a normal, healthy baby. But it doesn't end there.

The baby has got to reach the next level and develop sight and its ability to suck in order to eat. Now, if the baby is breathing and its heart is beating well, but it is not sucking properly, it will starve. So, you see, the struggle was not about just coming out of the mother's womb. That was only the beginning. The baby has to start functioning and cannot give up once one task is accomplished. The baby's bowels have got to move, air has got to hit its lungs. Every organ has got to be working. Just because the organs are working now does not mean that the struggle ceases or that the baby has reached its pinnacle of success. It has to keep going. Its brain has got to function and grow so that it can learn. Sicknesses must be overcome and germs must be warded off. Once the baby grows up, the challenges do not go away; they just change in nature.

Consider lions for a moment. A lion has got to train its cub how to live. It takes years before a cub learns how to hunt on its own, but it can never stop practicing. It play-fights with its siblings. It wrestles and learns how to use its teeth and claws to develop the hunting skills it will need in order to survive. Each cub undergoes the same process, otherwise it will fall prey to the wiles of the jungle.

This regimen is kept up until the cub's first hunt. Most likely, its first hunt will be a disaster. If so, then the cub must go without eating, because it failed to get the meal. But do you think they give up forevermore? No! They get back out there and try again. They have to keep at it until their hunting skills develop so greatly that they become master predators. No matter how sparse the pickings are, a lion will travel for miles in search of its next meal. It cannot afford to suffer defeat, because its entire existence relies on getting that next prey. If it gives up, it will become the prey instead of the predator.

We could learn a lot from the baby and the lion. You see, the day that we give up is the day that we become totally resigned to living in squalor and failure. As long as there is a struggle, then there is a spark of life. Without struggle, there is no fight left in the person because there are no more challenges.

Struggle is a combat and deals with two entities–good and the bad, right and the wrong, success and the failure. Struggle is a natural part of life and should not be viewed negatively. It makes life worth living.

8

THE FIGHT IS ON

*T*he key to winning every battle is knowing how to fight. Strategy! When I was growing up, my mother–being from Harlem, New York–instructed her children in the ways of battle. We were always told not to do a lot of talking when problematic situations arose. She taught us that most people who did a lot of talking before the fight didn't have time to think; so she taught us how to used that against our enemy.

While bullies made their braggadocios statements of what they were going to do and how they were going to do it, she taught us to be quiet, observe and find their weak spot. Right in the middle of their bragging and boasting of how they were going to hurt you, haul off and bust them in the bridge of their nose or any other place that would cause them to buckle and fall.

When they fell, she taught us to do whatever is necessary to make sure they don't get back up. Great motherly advice, huh? You better believe it. And if our opponent was too big, we were to get something in our hand and let that go to work for us.

The objective was to walk away from the fight that you didn't start, victoriously. The key was survival. She also had instructions for when you were accosted by more than one person. Those instructions were simply to focus on the leader of the gang and incapacitate him or her; for if you bring the leader down, the rest will scatter. Now that's unconventional teaching for children, but the principles behind my mother's strategy still stand true.

You see, if you won your battle, it was most likely that you wouldn't have to fight that type of battle again. And if by some chance you DID have to fight that battle again, you fought with the confidence and assurance that if you bested them once before, you could most likely do it again. So there was no fear of failure in that fight, only a sense of conquest. Why? Because you had proven that you had the power over your adversary.

There was another rule of battle in our family. This rule was that if one fights, we all had to fight! We had enough siblings in our family to assure that our battles would be brief and by reason of our numbers alone, we would be victorious. We never started a single fight, but we were prepared to finish them and finish them as VICTORS. You couldn't hit me without hitting my sisters; we were each other's greatest support. This may sound quiet violent and raucous, but sometimes it's those childhood experiences and analogies that will help us relate to the situations in our present and provide the strategies to overcome and secure our future.

Lest Satan should get an advantage of us: for we are not igno-rant of his devices. 2 Cor. 2:11

We lose many battles due to our IGNORANCE and IGNORING. Most regrettably, not only are we not aware of Satan's plans and tactics, but in many cases, we seem totally unconcerned. Let's take the two points that lead to certain defeat into consideration:

1. IGNORANCE–NOT KNOWING!!

In any professional fight, one of the main and most important things that a fighter does is sit, scrutinize and learn the ways of his opponent's fighting techniques. They cannot afford NOT to know. They use footage of his prior fights; they take notes of his strengths and his weaknesses. By they, I mean, the fighter along with his coach.

A coach is most important, for the coach will be a reminder, an instructor and director during the training, as well as the fight itself. While the fighter is in the midst of his battle, the coach will remind him of the things that he learned about his opponent during training that will give him the advantage and ultimately help him win the fight.

At all times, the fighter must be familiar with his opponent's strengths so that he may defensively counter them. He must also be aware of his opponent's weaknesses so that he may offensively take advantage of them and emerge from this fight, victorious. This victory is secured only by being alert, aware and prepared for your opponent.

2. IGNORING WHAT WE KNOW.

How many times have we run headlong into sin, broken hearts and failure simply because of a lack of prudence? I didn't say lack of wisdom; I said a lack of prudence. Now what is prudence? Prudence is not wisdom, but prudence is the practical application of wisdom. Simply put, we may be wise enough to know what's right and what's wrong. We know our weaknesses, what we should stay away from, who to stay away from and why to stay away, but if we do not apply that wisdom to our situations, we are guaranteed to fall and fail every time.

What's the good of knowing and not doing? Our failure, in this case, stems directly from the fact that we don't apply what we already know. We ignore the fact of our weakness–those same weaknesses that others will, undoubtedly, take advantage of.

Let me use this as an example:

Can a man take fire in his bosom, and his clothes not be burned? Proverbs 6:27

This simply asks if you can handle situations that you know you have a weakness for, and not be affected? Yet, some of us do it constantly. We ignore the fact that we have a weakness in our sexuality, then involve ourselves with people who keep us entangled in that weakness; all the while we'll declare until our fall, "I can handle it!" Ignoring the fact that this will only make our situation worse, we run headlong into a brick wall. Why? Because we ignored the weaknesses that we knew we had in our flesh and the tactics of the enemy to exploit that weakness.

In this fight for wholeness, the enemy is going to use every trick in the book to keep us bound to our past and rob us of our potential purpose, ultimately rendering us impotent so that we are not threat to him. Once we decide to move on from the paralyzing past and pain, and take on our potential purpose and overcome every obstacle, that's when our adversary unleashes everything that he can possibly find to keep us from our place of victory. The thoughts and memories and pains from our past will torment us; depression will try to seize our mind and our mind will become a major battlefield. But we have got to be determined–tenaciously determined–not just to fight, but to fight and win.

Fighting is inevitable in life. You cannot be afraid or withdraw from the struggles that come along with everyday existence. YOU WILL HAVE TO FIGHT! Whether you fight or not does not stop the war from going on. Those who do not fight when war is waged against them ultimately become savagely beaten and made servant and slave to their aggressor.

If you do not fight to overcome the problems of your past, you could become a slave to your past; given time, you will become comfortable in that slavery. My friend, that is not living; that is merely existing and that existence is quite miserable. Life is worth living and anything that is worth having is worth fighting for. So fight!

Fighting also means dealing with pain. Every blow delivered brings about some form of discomfort and pain. And being that we have inevitable pains in life anyway, we might as well suffer those pains, resist and overcome our past, and secure our futures. Let's face it... it's gonna hurt one way or the other. But what doesn't kill you can't help but make you stronger once you get the determination to fight. If I just have to suffer pain, I might as well suffer it fighting to win.

> *I therefore so run, not as uncertainly; so fight I, not as one that beateth the air: 1 Cor. 9:26*

We are not fighting just to fight and we're not fighting just to maintain. We are fighting to conquer our past, to revel and flourish in our present, and to gain a successful and prosperous future–body, mind, soul, spirit and life.

In the Christian belief, we have a tendency to give Satan too much credit. We give him credit for things that he doesn't have the power to do. In fact, we are guilty of making him larger than life. The Bible makes it plain that Satan doesn't have the power that he, and most of the Christian world, boast and believe that he has.

We blame him for everything that goes wrong in our lives. We hear it all of the time in our testimonies in church, and among ourselves. We constantly hear, "The devil this..." and "Satan that..." Those are the whinings of ignorant and childish "Christians". The true believer understands the power and authority that we wield through Jesus Christ.

We understand and stand firm in this fact:

> *Ye are of God, little children, and have overcome them: because greater is he that is in you, than he that is in the world.*
> *1 John 4:4*

We live by this Scripture:

No weapon that is formed against thee shall prosper; and every tongue that shall rise against thee in judgment thou shalt condemn. This is the heritage of the servants of the LORD, and their righteousness is of me, saith the LORD. Isaiah 54:17

What did Jesus say?

Behold, I give unto you power to tread on serpents and scorpions, and over all the power of the enemy: and nothing shall by any means hurt you. Luke 10:19

If this be true, then we have the power to conquer Satan, himself, through the authority of Jesus Christ, not to mention, handle the demons that are less than Satan in power. Satan can no longer be an excuse for our failure.

The real enemy–the most potent enemy–is OURSELVES. We have to live with ourselves everyday. We are the ones that allow ourselves to be reminded of and burdened with the hurt and problems, the past failures and the past abuses and fears. We are the ones who struggle with our memories, our feelings and our brokenness. We are the ones that accept the limitations imposed and enforced by our own insecurities. We are the ones that are our worst enemies! We have got to change "US!"

We have fear of the unknown. Our innermost desires, dreams and aspirations are held prisoner by this fear. We've got to FIGHT THE FEAR! You may not know your entire purpose, but don't let that stop you. Only YOU know what you truly have a passion for.

Granted, there may be a lot of things that you cannot do. But what is that one thing that you do well? That just may be the key to your purpose. Unlock it. Deal with and overcome your fears of doing it. Face your fear of not being as skilled as others. Fight each insecurity that feeds your reasons for remaining stagnant. Face those things head on. FIGHT THE FEAR!

Try in spite of your fear. And even when you fail–not if, but when you fail–get up and do the whole thing all over again. Find better ways to do it until you have success in that area. That is the only way to do it. You will never grow until you accept the challenge. Not just face it, but accept it. Purpose to overcome every challenge and come out VICTO-RIOUS!!

In order for me to pastor the church that God called me to pastor, I had to deal with my fear of not being adequate. I had to deal with my insecurities of thinking that I didn't have the biblical wisdom and prowess that so many of my contemporaries and predecessors have. I have been fortunate enough to interact with some of the great preachers of our era. How can I compete?

I don't think that I have ever been a part of an unsuccessful church or ministry. I clearly did not want to be the first. The "victim" in me still surfaces from time to time and causes me to say, "Lord, I can never do that. How in the world will I ever be able to be that good or that astute in the Bible? I can never be as great as this one... or that one. I will never measure up. I can't attain that level of excellence in my ministry. I CAN'T DO IT!"

Take Marvin Winans, for instance. That man preaches so well, he could probably preach in his sleep. Every Sunday, I would sit listening to him and wonder how could I ever keep up with him? He can take a subject, find Scriptures left and right and expound on them in a way that I have never heard anyone else do. Then, he has the nerve to come to me saying, "Donnie, you have got to do twice as much as I have. You have got to be greater than I am, otherwise, I have not done my job as a pastor." Talk about pressure! I would be totally intimidated because my fears were telling me that I could never be as good as he is.

I have traveled with Bishop T. D. Jakes. Everyone knows that Bishop Jakes has an awesome ability to use Scriptures and scenarios to deal with folks in their wounded state and get them to a point of wholeness. He ministers to almost 100,000 people in a setting. How can I ever measure up to him?

Fear says that I will never attain the level of others nor minister in the same magnitude, so why bother? Now, if I were to listen to those fears, I would call it quits. I chose, instead, to face all of those fears and conquer them before they conquered me. The truth is that I will never be able to do exactly what the others do. That's not my purpose or calling. I can only be who God purposed me to be and do what I've been born to do. So, I FIGHT THE FEAR.

When I'm among great men and women, I just sit there and learn. There's no need for me to pretend that I know it all, nor be intimidated by what I don't know. What I don't know, I make it my business to learn. I ask questions of those who are successful. I override my fear and sense of inferiority and glean from their experience.

Many people have been quite helpful, but I know that I had to be willing to first help myself. I had to apply what they told me. I had to spend time studying and learning and developing myself. If I surrender to my fears, then I'm doomed to failure. So, I FIGHT THE FEAR!

So, I'm encouraging you to RUN INTO THE CHALLENGE! Run into it, not away from it. Let me use another biblical example. King David will serve well here. When David was faced in battle with a great warrior named Goliath, most would have counted David out.

And it came to pass, when the Philistine arose, and came and drew nigh to meet David, that David hasted, and ran toward the army to meet the Philistine. And David put his hand in his bag, and took thence a stone, and slang it, and smote the Philistine in his forehead, that the stone sunk into his forehead; and he fell upon his face to the earth. 1 Samuel 17:48-49

David ran head long into the battle, knowing that he could and would conquer his fears and his foe. There are times when I feel like I'm dealing with a giant, especially when I do not know what is going to happen. I know that just by standing on the stage, I've made progress. Once I'm out there, I just tell myself, "Do what you've been purposed to do. Everything else will fall into place."

So, once you jump over those initial hurdles, you will find your God-given ability to not only begin, but also accomplish great things. With each success, no matter how small, comes a greater level of confidence, and that confidence will help you conquer fear every time. Are you willing to fight to make your greatness come through?

Change the way you think and how you view yourself, and see yourself as Christ sees you; you will have many more victories.

In Christ, we are VICTORIOUS! We are OVERCOMERS! We are MORE THAN CONQUERORS! The battle is already won and the fight has been fixed. The end has already been determined, if we will follow the instructions of our Coach, The Holy Spirit!

9

BROKEN

*T*here's a song that I sing that says, "We fall down, but we GET UP!" Well at least some of us get up again, while others chose to sit and wallow in the mud of their hurt and despair. They are "broken!" For the victim, brokenness is not easily remedied. The longer you stay in the state of brokenness, the harder your heart becomes, or the more the depression grows and the abuse is repeated. When you're broken, you begin to operate in bitterness, resentment, addictions and unforgiveness towards others as well as yourself.

Unforgiveness is like a death sentence the victim renders upon himself, committing him to the confines of his own personal hell. Bitterness slows a person down and hinders progress. It causes us to propel our anger—anger with the things that have gone wrong—onto innocent people because issues have gone unresolved.

If we do not address the issues surrounding our victimization, we will harbor unforgiveness and latent self-hatred;

we'll soon develop destructive habits, thus affecting our minds and the very way that we live.

When neglected, rejected, or abused in our formative years, we develop mentalities that are seemingly always in search of affirmation, validation and love in all of the wrong places. This broken mentality ultimately leads to further abuse, rejection and neglect.

How many people, in search of love, have given themselves, sexually, away, just to be humiliated, betrayed and left in a worse condition than when they began? How many endure and settle for humiliating and demeaning words or physical and mental abuse in their quest for true love; all the while they are believing, with broken spirits, that this is all that they're worth and the best that they can do?

I realize that people differ and that this may not hold true for everyone. However, the way one deals with a situation has a huge bearing on how, and with what quality, they live their lives. Left unchecked, unforgiveness will become like a "monkey on their back." It will become a part of life–a little extension of existence.

Many people think that I would be quite justified if I hated my uncle and others that abused and misused me. After all, I did not choose to be raped and molested. But then there's a question that I had to address: What about the choices that I made since being an adult?

I was the one that accepted a destructive mindset. When I didn't consciously counter those dysfunctional thoughts, they grew from thoughts to desires, and from desires to actions. Those actions, birthed from my dysfunctional thoughts, led to perversion that affected and infected my lifestyle. But once I realized all of this, it was my obligation to change my thinking and actions, deliberately.

I realized that I had the opportunity and capability to stop the destructive process. I decided to deal with the pain of overcoming my addictions. You see, I was dealing with more than a mere desire; it became a full-blown addiction. I came to finally understand that in order to overcome this addictive pattern and lifestyle, it was going to take a real effort on my part to break this, completely.

> *For to be carnally minded* [led by your lusts, sins, addictions and inordinate passions] *is death; but to be spiritually mind-ed* [led by the Divine Spirit given to you by God] *is life and peace.*   Romans 8:6

Our quest for life and peace has to begin in the most important battleground: Our mind! Our lusts, sins, addictions and inordinate passions cause us to be separated from our God-ordained purpose and effectiveness. Those secret struggles and things–that are never dealt with, hidden away to be done in secret–will disrupt and ultimately be seen in your lifestyle, in one manner or another.

Rest assured in this fact in the Bible:

> *But if ye will not do so, behold, ye have sinned against the LORD: and be sure your sin will find you out [or one day be seen]. Numbers 32:23*

I know that the word "sin" is usually used exclusively in the religious circles, but it must be included in these equations, as well.

Sin is anything that is against nature and against God–anything morally or spiritually wrong. For example, tobacco, in and of itself, is not evil and harmful. It is of no danger to anyone until it is abnormally used. Only after chemicals are added to it and once it's rolled, lit and/or inhaled into your lungs does its harmful carcinogens cause emphysema and cancer. That's abuse (ABnormal USE)!

The transgression is committed once the natural use of something is altered. In our brokenness, we can allow our-selves to be used in some very abusive manners. I was broken by the sexual violation that happened to me. My uncle used me in an abnormal way, and, thus, it caused me to function, sexually, in a broken manner.

The abnormal use of my sexuality continued until I came to realize that I was broken and that homosexuality was not God's intention and divine method and purpose for my masculinity. This was ABnormal USE of my manhood. My biology and anatomy was not made for that type of usage. It wasn't just a godly law, but there was a NATURAL law that was being broken. And no matter what others said or how "right" it felt emotionally and physically, as with the tobacco, this also had a harmful result. The same is true for those in heterosexual ABUSE.

So, as with any bone that's been broken and not prop-erly treated, it will mend, but it's usage will be limited and never with the fluid dexterity that was intended. The bone must be broken and reset, properly, in order for it to heal cor-rectly and be used to its fullest extent and potential.

The same is true of our lives. Even though the pain is gone and we've grown comfortable in the broken lifestyle and can function enough to live, our lives are still deformed. Our lives will remain deformed until we allow God to reset us for normal and intended use.

So, in the battle that I had to fight, the only way for me to start the healings and gain the victory was to uncover the things that I fought with in secret and lay them out on the table–to allow them to be brought to the forefront. I had to be willing to endure whatever it took for me to be entirely whole again.

There is a dark side of man we fight, constantly, to overcome. A side that wants its own way and wants to fulfill its own pleasures. It's in everyone! A side that does not want to submit to God. A side that ignores morality and abandons righteousness. A side that causes us to throw caution to the wind and just give in to what we know is wrong. That carnal lifestyle separates us from our relationship with and purpose in God. It leads to death in a spiritual sense.

The more we give into this broken living, the more desensitized we become to those things that are wrong we become more apt to give in again with less resistance. The brokenness will continue until we determine to make a change.

Deal with the truth about yourself. The only way you will ever achieve total wholeness is by confronting YOUR TRUE SELF–your addictions and habits, your mindset and your actions. It's time for real repairs.

You may have spent a lifetime absolving yourself of any responsibility for your behavior. You may have grown accustomed to blaming your deeds on your upbringing and on others. But, regardless of the original cause, YOU are the one living with the effects. You have to have your life repaired. Don't allow your purpose to be lost just because your innocence was stolen.

Deal with the whole you, not just with what happened to you in the past. Allow the complete YOU to be healed, mended and put back together.

10

BREAK THE CYCLE

*R*ape and sexual abuse do not just happen with children, though they are usually the most helpless victims to be violated. I remember talking with a 44-year old woman who has grown children. She had been date raped by a brother from her church. Not only was she traumatized; she was also victimized twice—sexually and socially.

She felt like she could not even speak to her pastor about the matter. For weeks, she went around unable to tell anyone. She couldn't sleep at night because she would relive the moment over and over again in her mind. She finally went back to church. Imagine the pain of having to see that brother there, knowing that if you said a word about what happened, no one would believe you.

Here she was a lonely, 44-year old, divorced woman with grown children. She had invited the brother into her home late at night. Clearly everyone would have believed she asked for it, or so she thought. Unfortunately, that is just what predators, like that brother, bank on. If a woman lets her guard down and invites a man into her home, he knows that there is a good chance people will not believe her. He feeds on her fears of being rejected by society, assaults her, and gets away, virtually "scott-free".

You know what is crazy? Some church folks might tell that woman to just forget about what happened–as though that were possible. That woman was victimized, raped, humiliated, and violated in the worse way. Do you really think she's just going to forget all about that? No!

I told her to go to the police, because if he did it then, who knows if he's done it before. But it's a good bet he will do it again. No one would be that brave to rape someone without having done it before. He would have had to over-ride some serious mental blocks, moral blocks, and spiritual blocks in order to violate someone in such an angry, aggressive manner and feel no remorse.

So, you know what? Help him out. Help him to not commit that crime against someone else's daughter. Make sure that it doesn't happen to another child or cause someone else to feel dirty, as though they did something to merit such an attack. By going to the police, you are saving someone else from imminent harm, hurt, and danger.

Whatever recourse the law has for that offender–whether it is counseling or jail time–you will not be the victim again, because you did not keep quiet. You were a victim of the violation, but became a victor, in spite of the situation.

Break the cycle of abuse. Whether you are a young person or an adult, if you have been victimized, tell someone who it was that violated you and when it happened. Was it someone in your family? One woman told me her sister sexually abused her as a child.

Like I told her, if there are issues that have not been dealt with, sit with the family, pray about it, or talk to someone, but don't allow it to just fester inside of you. If it's troubling you and has you traumatized, even now that you're older, sit down and speak with somebody about it. Get professional counseling, either clinically or clergically.

Open up the wound and let it heal properly. Be prepared, because it may cause division in your family. A lot of people will wonder why you waited so long before speaking up. Let them know that you waited because you have been living in your own private hell all of these years with the memory of it and feeling as though you had no one to confide in. Just to cope, you acted as though it never happened; wishing that you could eventually fool yourself into believing it was all just a nightmare.

My friend, open up. Tear down the walls you've placed around your heart. Talk to someone. Tell a minister. Seek counseling. Inform someone. If it is still happening, run and get help. Don't suffer in silence. You can have power over the situation. Being a victim is not your destiny.

Take the power out of the hand of the one who hurt you. Take the control away from the one who preyed upon you. Just tell someone. Stop the abuse. Tell whomever you have to tell and write whomever you have to write to prevent it from happening again. You will only damage yourself by letting it continue. You have to tell somebody.

Darkness hates the light and thrives on secrecy. As long as you remain silent, you allow the evil to continue lurking in the shadows. Not saying anything sanctions it to not only happen again, but to be more aggressive, violent, and perverse the next time. Each time the crime is committed, the criminal has less and less conviction.

The first time they did it, they were probably appalled by their propensity to do such an evil thing. The second time, they may have felt they were hurting someone, but they didn't feel as bad. By the third time, they were just perfecting their skill. They flourish on your silence. It increases their chances to be able to inflict harm again.

Kill their chances by disclosing what happened. Bring their darkness into the light. If they deny it to the hilt, your revelation of what happened will cause them to be cautious and hesitant. Even if they say you are lying, doubt will be placed in the minds of others, and people will be more careful to watch the perpetrator. They will no longer have the freedom to go unchallenged in the abuse.

Now, there'll be a record somewhere—not just with mom and dad, but also with the police. Even if the worst case scenario proves to be true and you lose your case in court, a record of your complaint will be filed. So, should the perpetrator ever do it again, there will be a report on file that can be used against the person.

You see, if you do not catch him, he will strike again. Your report can save somebody else's son or daughter, mother or father, or sister or brother from the depravity of that perpetrator.

The only way to stop his vicious cycle of abuse is to sound the alarm by opening your mouth and revealing what happened. That is the only way to not only save others from experiencing the heartache you had to suffer, but also to help the perpetrator. That's right; help the perpetrator, because they will never help or tell on themselves. They will only help themselves to abusing someone else.

Free yourself of the guilt. Free yourself of the secrecy and the shame. Open up so that you can be healed. Even if your family fights to keep those skeletons in the closet, it is too heavy a load to bear by yourself.

Tell somebody. If it was your father that committed unspeakable atrocities against you, tell someone. It doesn't matter if you are grown now and have your own children, tell somebody because you don't know who your father is still abusing. Perhaps your child will be next.

Maybe your mother abused you. Again, tell somebody. If your abuser can ever be in a position to hurt someone else, you owe it to yourself to ensure that no one else ever has to go through the hell you went through. Make sure it never happens to any of your children, nieces or nephews, or any-body else's children.

Even if the perpetrator is old and gray, they cannot be trusted, especially if you never told anyone what happened. The problem is not going to just fade away because the per-son's sexual libido has waned. They have an addiction, and it has nothing to do with sexual drive. It is a sick problem, and even if the person cannot perform sexually, their addiction will still cause them to accost in whatever way they can and damage lives.

Have nothing to do with the fruitless deeds of darkness, but rather expose them. Ephes. 5:11 NIV

11

PROTECT THE CHILDREN

*O*ftentimes, when someone grows up in a dys-functional home, and either the mom or dad was not there, imbalance occurs. I personally know of many single-parent homes where mothers are doing their best to raise their child by themselves.

Despite their most valiant efforts, one person cannot see or be everything. It takes two parents. I know that may be an unpopular thing to assert in today's society, but a mother can never be both mother and father. She can only be the moth-er and try to fill in the gaps here and there. Likewise, a father cannot fill the shoes of a mother by himself.

A father gives a boy his purpose. Fathers give their girls security. If the father is a real man—not just a real male—then, he will be the male blueprint his son can follow and the kind of man his daughter will want to marry. A husband that treats his wife right is always a hero to his daughter and a viable role model for his son.

I have a two-year-old nephew that sticks to me like glue. One day as I was preparing for a trip, I finally realized just how much attention kids pay to adults. We are a profound influence in their lives. We help to mold them, not only by what we say, but, more importantly, by what we do. As I was packing my bags, my nephew came into my room and said, "Uncle Donnie, I need a bag. I need a bag." So, I gave him a little cologne bag.

While I was putting my clothes into my bag, he began putting things into his little bag. I took the wire from my computer and started wrapping it up so that I could put it in my computer case. All of a sudden, he needed a wire too. I handed him a cord, and he started wrapping it up the same way I was. I packed up, got my bag and was walking down the stairs when I noticed him tugging along his little bag right behind me. I put my bag down, sat on the stairs, and folded my arms. Needless to say, he put his bag down, folded his little arms, and sat right next to me.

All at once, it hit me! That is where the learning begins. At two years old, he will probably never remember doing that, but his psyche had already caused him to develop traits of masculinity just from being around a male figure. He was emulating my masculinity. He was incorporating my actions into his behavior. My manhood was affecting him and giving him a template on which to record how to be a man.

My nephew, his sister (she's five years older than him), and their mother (my sister), all live with me. My sister is divorced. In our home, I became like a father figure to my niece and nephew; I take on the role to cover and protect them, as a father should.

We monitor what they watch and do not allow them to watch MTV, VH1, or BET music videos. They don't listen to secular music in our home. They attend Christian schools. When they visit their friend's house, we ask their friend's parents to reinforce our guidelines in their home while my niece and nephew are visiting. The daycare worker knows to only play gospel music around them. We have made sure to cover as many bases as possible so as to ward out possible entries for the enemy to come in and pervert their minds.

We watch those kids like a hawk. If they exhibit strange behavior, we can usually narrow it down to where they picked it up. For instance, when my niece was five years old, she used to like showing her stomach to everybody by lifting up her shirt. We wondered where she got that. We addressed it with her daycare giver and others until we found out where my niece learned to do that. We did not just overlook it and assume my niece was just acting like a little girl. She was acting just like someone she had seen. It was a learned response, not a natural one.

Fathers, in particular, need to return to their children. Even if they are not married to their children's mother, they really need to play an active role in their child's life. Children need to reap the benefits of being around both their mother and father. Fathers, care for your children, regardless of the circumstances that surrounded their conception or birth. Fail not to instill within your son the principles of manhood–character, integrity, ethics, and respect.

Help your son establish his identity. Don't let him guess at it. If you fail to be an influence in your child's life, believe me, someone else will fill that task—whether good or bad. Television personalities will influence you children if you leave them in front of the tube. Music will have that same influence. Less than favorable role models will have that same influence, whether they are gay or heterosexual.

Children are like blank slates and are very impressionable. As a parent, I would not allow my children to be taught the rainbow curriculum in school. The rainbow curriculum teaches children homosexual ideals and describes "families" that consist of two lesbian mothers or two homosexual fathers. When children are taught those things at such tender, young ages, they begin to form belief systems that accept homosexuality as a natural lot in life.

You do not have to sit idly by and let your children integrate carnal viewpoints into their lives. Allow them to be innocent and have a happy childhood, no matter what is going on in society. I know I want my children to be whole and to grow up, be productive, and have their own families. Consequently, I have to fight against things that are made to deter them from their purpose and the will of God for their lives.

How do you protect your children from predators? Simple! Don't let them leave your side. In church, let them sit next to you. If you don't know the director or who teaches in the children's programs, then do not entrust your children to them. Furthermore, don't send them to the bathroom alone.

Behold, I send you forth as sheep in the midst of wolves: be ye therefore wise as serpents, and harmless as doves.

Matthew 10:16

My mother never let her children go anywhere without her. When we were old enough to go to the bathroom alone, she would still stand outside of the bathroom door and wait for us to come out. We never spent the night at anyone's home. It was not even feasible for my mother to not know where her children were or what they were doing.

All of my years growing up, my mother told us point blank, "Don't you ever let me see you walking with anybody that you don't know, even if they tell you I told them to come and get you. Don't you ever let me see you talking to a stranger. And, I better not catch you in somebody else's car." I'm telling you, we would have gotten beat to death if she thought we accepted a ride from a stranger.

Even if we were with a bunch of friends and someone offered us a ride, we would decline and just let them know we would rather walk. Our mother had us so timed that she knew exactly how long it should take for us to get home. Day in and day out, we could count on her to be standing at the window waiting to see us coming down the street.

That's just something mothers did back in the day. Children were not left to fend for themselves. They were under the constant care of their parents.

I remember we could not even go outside without asking first. Our mother would always tell us to stay in the yard where she could see us. She wasn't being mean. She was being protective. She did not want to take a chance on having something happen to us.

Shield your children from the hands of those that would only mean to harm them. You want your children to be outgoing and personable to a certain degree, but in this society, you have to be cautious with your most prized possession—your children.

You have to be careful that their exuberance and outgoing personality do not cause them to befriend the wrong person. Sometimes you have to put a harness on that. You've got to revert back to the old school way of doing things and not let your children—your greatest gift in the world—out of your sight, until you know that they are ready to handle the world and all of its vices by themselves.

The only way a predator can gain entrance to your family is when someone is sleeping. Someone has to neglect watching. Because of the fear my mother instilled in me about strangers, I was not susceptible to the ploys of an outsider. The abuse I went through was because of an uncle and his son, not a stranger. It happened during a time when my mother was in a haze from losing my brother. She and my father were estranged at the time.

Had circumstances been different, my uncle would never have been able to even get close to me, let alone violate me in such a way. If my brother had not died, that whole chapter in my life would be nonexistent. You see, he was just like other predators, waiting in the wings for that one moment of neglect, when somebody lets their guard down.

Predators can sense the prime moment to strike. Oh, they are patient and know just when to hit quickly and quietly.

When it comes to your child, you cannot be overprotective. I'm not talking about hiding behind bushes and not trusting the child; I'm talking about making the concerted effort to safeguard them. I know I want to make every effort to make sure that what happened to me does not happen to my child. I may have been a victim, but my greatest job is to make sure that is not passed down to my child.

My children and my children's children should never have to go through what I experienced in any shape, form or fashion. It ends with me. I am the Joseph. I suffered the abuse, but after me, it ends. Now, righteousness, peace, and joy will be passed on to my children, and as long as I can help it, they will never have to suffer the way I did.

I will be their protector, their guardian, and their safeguard. I will be the example and prototype my children can follow. My son will be whole and healthy in every area of his life. My daughter will be a great woman, unashamed of exhibiting her femininity. Their lives are worth whatever extra energy I have to go through to make sure they are safe.

12

I NEED YOU

I know that one of the premises of this book is to help people break their dependencies on other people, and to move on with a full and happy life. So then, why a chapter that seems to foster dependency? Because the truth is that we cannot live a happy and fulfilled life alone.

I know, we've heard it a thousand times from people who have had horrific relationships that left them scarred say, "I don't need anybody! I can make it with just ME, MYSELF, AND I!" Those are just empty words from a wounded heart.

Even in the church, we've lamented over hurts and broken and failed relationships, and written songs that are totally asinine and untrue, and passed them off as GOSPEL songs; when, in fact, they're songs that display our dysfunctional outlook on life and interaction with others. One song, in particular, comes to mind: A song that states, "Long as I got Jesus, I don't need NOBODY else!" (Excuse the bad grammar.)

Now, that's nowhere near true, and it's not what God intended. God put us here with too many other people for us to believe that all that we need is Jesus, and absolutely NO ONE else. The song says, "I don't need my mother." Then, without her, how are were you born? "I don't need my father." Then there is no seed of you to be born. "I don't need my sister or brother." Then the Bible is wrong:

A friend loveth at all times, and a brother is born for adversity. Proverbs 17:17

The song goes on to say, "I don't need a doctor." Then, you're going to die sick. "I don't need a lawyer." Then, if anything legal arises, you'll have to represent yourself; and the adage says, "He who represents himself in a court of law, has a fool for a client!"

Then the song says something that causes me great concern. It states, "I don't need a preacher, or a teacher!" How is that possible as a Christian that you don't need a preacher or a teacher? The Bible says otherwise:

How then shall they call on him in whom they have not believed? and how shall they believe in him of whom they have not heard? and how shall they hear without a preacher? Romans 10:14

Why do we perpetuate this dysfunctional mentality even in our churches? The most miserable people that you could ever find are the ones who have cut themselves off from friends, family, and people, in general. They have to become calloused and develop an "I don't care" attitude in order to disconnect from their natural need to give and receive love, and in order to cover the brokenness, within. That is not living. That is merely existing. But in order to be totally victorious, we need to know that it's got to be together. As ONE!

Everything that is in existence today is made up of a series of multiples. Nothing that has ever been created exists alone without any support. Our nine planets, with their several moons, orbiting around the sun, make up ONE solar system. One hundred and fifty million stars and planets make up ONE universe. Over 200 billion stars make up ONE galaxy. A series of multiples. One atom, that is the make-up of all matter, is made up of THREE parts: proton, neutron, and the electron. One atom–three parts. Everything that is, needs something else in order to exist.

The Bible addresses this in Ecclesiastes:

Two are better than one; because they have a good reward for their labour. Eccles. 4:9

Alone, we remain with our victim's mentality, throwing a pity party that no one else wants to attend, and sitting behind a wall that we've built–a wall so high that no one else can get to us. But when you have friends, they love you, regardless of what you've done, where you've been, or who you are. If you fall victim to your past again, a friend and/or family member will not allow you to suffer through it alone. A friend will aid you in your time of trouble.

But now are they many members, yet but one body. And the eye cannot say unto the hand, I have no need of thee: nor again the head to the feet, I have no need of you. Nay, much

more those members of the body, which seem to be more fee-
ble, are necessary: And those members of the body, which we
think to be less honourable, upon these we bestow more abun-
dant honour; and our uncomely parts have more abundant
comeliness. For our comely parts have no need: but God hath
tempered the body together, having given more abundant hon-
our to that part which lacked: That there should be no schism
in the body; but that the members should have the same care
one for another. And whether one member suffer, all the
members suffer with it; or one member be honoured, all the
members rejoice with it. 1 Cor. 12:20-26

The problem lies in the fact that in order to trust, you have to make yourself VULNERABLE! I know that is a word and concept that may bring fear to some. Most of us don't like to think about ever being that way again. We've made the statements, "I'll never let anyone get that close to me again!" or "I will never allow myself to love like that again!" But in order to live, you have to love and trust all over again.

You have to let your guard down, to a certain extent, and allow yourself to include others in your "world" again. And I know that it wouldn't be so hard if one question was asked and proven: "Can I trust you?" That's the thing most folk who have been deeply wounded want to know: "CAN I TRUST YOU?"

Can I trust you with my life? Can I trust that you'll cover me when I'm wrong and not have you offer what you know of me up on the altars of gossip? Can I trust you to cover me from the rubbernecks that slow up at the scene of my accident, not necessarily to help out, but just to say that they actually saw it for themselves?

That's the main thing that I need to know. I need you to stand in the gap for me when I've fallen. I need for you to challenge and resist every enemy that comes against me when I'm down and I need to know that you'll fight for me, just as I will for you.

I need for you to tell my enemy, "Before you get to my friend, you've got to go through me, first!" I need you and you need me. I'm crazy enough to believe that there are some people out there who will be just that type of friend, just as I would be to them. They may be few and far between, but I do believe that they exist.

I want to address the "church" for a moment on how it handles victims. What I am referring to is not the church that the Bible speaks of, but the religious sect and community that exemplifies religious practices and traditions, but not real, godly love. They have a knowledge of God, but, somehow, fail to show His true love in their interactions with others.

The religious community becomes abusive when they lack true compassion and tolerance for humankind. Everyone has a vice of some sort. At times, the religious community becomes a little too dogmatic and sometimes, fails to embrace the very ones the church was meant to embrace.

The world does not trust the church any more because "religious" people have made it such an exclusive "country club" type experience; "outsiders" feel as if they have to walk, talk, dress, act and think like "us" in order to be accepted. People are made to feel as though they have to pass some type of denominational litmus test in order to be welcomed.

Consequently, the church winds up not helping the very people it was created to help–those who have be victimized by sin, victimized by society, victimized by people, and even victimized by their own self-hatred and low self-esteem.

How hurting it is for someone to turn to the church, the last bastion of hope, only to face rejection there, too. People are hurting and in need of acceptance and true healing. They have been wounded by their past and come to church in search of viable answers to life's difficult questions.

In their search for a merciful and loving Savior and loving people, they hear things, instead, like what they cannot wear into the church and how they cannot wear their hair. Unfortunately, these things still go on in some churches.

People go through their own personal "hell"; the place that they are supposed to be able to run to–the church–and find hope and help, sometimes fails in offering true hope and help. We must revisit and re-evaluate the role of the church. It is not to act as the spiritual "bully" on the block, but the haven of love and help.

This is not an indictment on the true church and body of Christ, nor the true ministries–large or small–that are helping and healing the masses. This is just to remind some of us that the church's job is to embrace all kinds of people and share the unconditional love of Jesus Christ. It's to reach out to those who have been wounded, bruised by life and hurting, and–remembering ourselves when we were a mess and needed help–love them back to wholeness.

If we could develop that type of mindset and relation-ship, we would salvage so many people from some hellish ordeals. I would hate to live this life alone. I love people and it's always good to know that some people love me, too.

13

Do Something About It!

I have spent many years mulling over the things that have gone on in my life and sometimes I had the tendency to look back, retrospectively, and lament over the things that I could have accomplished, but haven't.

I focused on the education that I could have finished; the music that I could have studied and learned; the relationships that I could have had; the monies that I could have made, kept, and increased if I only had the discipline that I needed. And the list goes on and on.

What an absolute waste of good time! Just thinking about it didn't do me any good, whatsoever. It only made me all the more depressed. But thank God for good friends who would not let me hold on to that victim's mentality around them. Friends who gave me "hard love" and wouldn't allow me to lick my wounds and sing the "Woe is Me" song.

I had friends that would listen, understand, work with me and sympathize to a certain extent. Then, once they saw me leaning too heavily on their sympathy, cut me off, to a degree and tell me, "Stop crying! Stop making excuses! Stop kvetching (yiddish for "griping")! Do something about it!"

Sympathy has its limits. People will listen and go with you only so far if you refuse to move on. And I discovered that once you develop a comfort and safety zone in your dilemma, it becomes quite difficult to break free of that, and move on. Again, difficult, but not impossible. Like I stated in one of the chapters before, I'm not able nor am I attempting to give you clinical advice on how to break free of this type of situation, but I can share with you how I broke the pattern in my life and moved on to wholeness.

Being around strong-willed people used to always intimidate me in the worst way. My inadequacies were always magnified to me when interacting with self-assured, productive men. In many ways, the intimidation was crippling.

I would be afraid to perform in any way before them, convinced that I couldn't measure up to their standards. Embarrassed by my totally inept athleticism in the presence of their stat-quoting displays. Watching them play sports that I've already convinced myself that I'd suck at (excuse my language) if I tried to learn or join in.

I couldn't bring myself to sing around them, because I was convinced that they were all far better singers than I could ever be. Wouldn't play the piano with them, knowing that my talent was so under-par. Wouldn't let them hear the songs that I wrote, because they were accomplished songwriters and artists with many credits and awards to their name. And after all, who would want to hear my songs?

But these were not the type of friends that would let you live like that around them. They would push you. They would encourage you. They would include you in their conversations. Although they would laugh at your lack of knowledge and athletic ability in sports, they would also help you learn, even though they wouldn't let you be on their softball team during the annual church picnic. It was really a "skin-toughener" being around them.

To break those insecurities, I made it my point of business to stay in those uncomfortable environments where I could learn and OVERRIDE my fear of failure by learning what I didn't know. Now, it's not an easy thing to just "up" and start doing something that you feel inadequate in doing. It takes some real tenacity to get out of that "I don't measure up" rut. It was a few years before I realized the progress that I was making, and the self-worth I was developing. But God knows, it was worth it.

What I didn't have, I went and got. I faced what I was afraid of, and painfully worked on that until I overcame it. What I was convinced that I couldn't do or learn, I applied myself to and gradually acquired it and put it to use for me. I made myself become informed about things that seemed beyond my grasp of understanding by reading and reading. No time for crying and licking wounds. It's time for action.

For years, I was afraid to take on the responsibilities of adult life and lived in a very limited world of meager existence. Afraid of having to do things without help and afraid to admit what I didn't know and ask for help to learn what I needed to learn.

I lived with a friend for a few months and vicariously lived a pseudo-maturity through him. I became dependent upon he and his wife without even realizing it.

For four months I slept in their home, ate their food, live with them as one of the family until reality hit me square in the chest. THIS WAS NOT MY HOME!!!!! How did I come to this epiphany? It was easy! I was asked to LEAVE!!!!! I was ever so nicely EVICTED from their home. My friend had a nice conversation with me and let me know that I had two weeks to find a place of my own. It was the best thing in the world to happen to me, as I look back in retrospect.

The dependency that I was allowing to develop was only crippling me and assuring that I would never progress to the place of maturity that a man should reach. For the first time in my life, I had to do something totally on my own. I had to make my own way and be the sole provider for myself. I had to get that job cleaning toilets in the Mercy Family Care Clinic and make minimum wage washing down lice-ridden examination rooms and disposing of syringes and blood vials from infected HIV patients. I counseled the distraught, in between cleanings, all for just $120.00 a week.

But I had to do something about my present situation in order to live—no matter how menial the task. I had to stick with it until something better came along. No more excuses. I was responsible for my own progress and success.

The saying goes, "A man (or woman) has got to do what a man (or woman) has got to do!" If you hide from the realities and responsibilities of life, you condemn yourself to a non-productive existence.

Just because you've been bad with money management in the past doesn't mean that you have to resign yourself to being broke and without. It simply means that you have to learn–no matter how grueling–and discipline yourself to adopt a frugal mindset in order to live a prosperous life of security and comfort.

Push yourself to learn what you don't know and to do what you should be doing. It will make all the difference in the world and change your life, as you know it. But it doesn't just come by luck. It doesn't just manifest out of thin air and appear out of nothing. It's not something that materializes just because you wish for, hope for, and expect it. That's FANTASY!

Let me speak to the church people for just one moment, again. There's a stark difference between FAITH and FANTASY. Sometimes in the church world, we get those two confused and suffer a lot of disappointments as a result. We testify that God is going to provide and make a way for us. We tell others that God's going to give us everything that we need if we just wait on Him and that's just what we do. We shut down and WAIT! We do nothing and WAIT! We make no efforts whatsoever and WAIT!!! That is not faith, that's FANTASY. True faith is always accompanied by action.

Even so faith, if it hath not works, is dead, being alone. Yea, a man may say, Thou hast faith, and I have works: shew me thy faith without thy works, and I will shew thee my faith by my works. Thou believest that there is one God; thou doest well: the devils also believe, and tremble. But wilt thou know, O vain man, that faith without works is dead? Was not Abraham our father justified by works, when he had offered Isaac his son upon the altar? Seest thou how faith wrought with his works, and by works was faith made perfect? And the scripture was fulfilled which saith, Abraham believed God, and it was imputed unto him for righteousness: and he was called the Friend of God. Ye see then how that by works a man is justified, and not by faith only. Likewise also was not Rahab the harlot justified by works, when she had received the messengers, and had sent them out another way? For as the body without the spirit is dead, so faith without works is dead also.

James 2:17-26

You see, faith is not believing in some mystical fantastic happening of the magical nature. Faith is not believing in something that is NOT THERE. Faith is believing and KNOWING that whatever God has planned for you ALREADY IS!! Just because you can't see it right now doesn't mean that it's not there. Just because it hasn't manifested yet doesn't mean that it isn't so. Just because you can't see your help doesn't mean that it's not there for you.

Faith says, "God cannot be wrong! I am what and who God says that I am! I have what and ALL that God says that I can have!" Time will not deter my determination nor will I change my confession because of it. I will not just sit by, idly twiddling my thumbs, waiting for something to "miraculously" drop from the sky. I will apply myself. I will pool my resources and bring all of my God-given talents and abilities to bear as I move on what and who God has said that I am.

I can do all things through Christ which strengtheneth me.
Philip. 4:13

My brother Tony on his tricycle at age 4

My Dad at work with his backhoe. 1970

My father and Tony

Tony at age 5

Donny at age 10, holding Tony (5 months old)

My grandmother, Olivia Jenkins.
What a remarkable resemblance between
my grandmother and great grandmother!

My great grandmother, Mary Dinge. 1940

Donnie playing piano, age 17.

Donnie at age 17, my sister Andrea at age 14

Tony and my sister Marlene. 1985

Mom & Dad, stop that!
That's how you got all those children!

Donnie – Eternal Victor!

14

FINALLY LETTING IT GO

*T*his is a tough one. It isn't as easy as it's portrayed to be. Letting go of memories, feelings, hurts and anger is not a simple task. You can't wipe clean all of the remembrances and images that haunt and torment. The words that wounded you so deeply and the rejection that scarred your emotions so badly are not that easily dismissed.

Some of us still have to deal with not only the memories, but also the yet living victimizers, themselves. They serve as the constant reminder of the hellish ordeal. Sometimes the pain and hurt is too real to just ignore. I understand.

I receive e-mails from around the world and the majority of them deal with being broken by a loved one or relative. One woman in particular, was raped by her father throughout her childhood and at 16 years old gave birth to her father's child. Her mother was there for all of those years, yet the incestuous abuse continued.

Just tell me this... How does a mother NOT KNOW that her child is being abused? That, I just cannot and will not understand. How does a mother NOT see the light of childhood innocence fade and die? How can the family not see the pain and turmoil in the eyes of the precious, silent victim?

Her father threatened her for years and told her that if she told anyone at anytime, he would kill her. Now, as an adult, she has lost her family because she chose to reveal it in counseling sessions. Her siblings are enraged, concerned only about what would be thought of the family once this was exposed. But what about the hell of silence and the torture of having to still hide after all of these years.

After all of the hell of growing up in this violating abuse and having to be victimized in silence, now some twenty years later, she is still being victimized by the her family into silence. Left alone to raise the child born of incest and be reminded every time she looks at the child of the horrid ordeals forced on her by her own father. How does one handle that?

This is where I have to end my advice giving and pass this sister on to professional help. Whether clergy or clinical, there is a lot of mental help needed. But the only focus and goal is to be able to let all of the garbage and baggage of the past go and allow the healing to begin.

Throughout this book, I try not to be too flippant and arrogantly presumptuous in anything that I say or advise, or any Scripture that I give. We all have to take into account that everyone's situation differs and in some of these cases "one size doesn't always fit all!" If one mode of help doesn't work, find another, without hesitation. For the only thing that matters is finally being able to let our past go and move on to a whole and happy future.

Now allow me, for a few moments, to make this clear... and I may anger some folk with this statement but it's nonetheless true. The religious community is neither always able nor equipped to adequately deal with some of the problematic situations that people are dealing with in today's dramatic and traumatic society. Things that were pushed under the carpet years ago have got to be dealt with head on today. We, in the religious community, have got to know our limitations and not try to counsel in areas that we are not qualified in because BAD help is sometimes worse than no help at all.

If a person's situation is beyond our scope of knowledge or expertise, pass them on to some profession that will be able to help and bring that person into wholeness. For it really doesn't matter how the help comes about, it's just important that it DOES come about.

I had an in-depth conversation with a friend of mine who works in a religious helps and assistance program for young pre-teen and teenage girls dealing with the issues of pregnancy and such matters. We began to talk about a pre-teen that was impregnated by her father and was faced with either aborting the child or keeping the child and having the pre-teen endure nine months of carrying a child sired by her own father. Not to mention the fact that the pre-teen would have to have to raise the constant reminder of her father's perverse dysfunction and her total loss of childhood innocence.

My friend spouted out advice that was harsh and callous, declaring that the pre-teen girl should be made to have the child in order to preserve the life of the unborn. Regardless of how it will scar and damage the child carrying the child... regardless of the profound physical and mental handicap that the doctors said would result. Because of RELIGIOUS beliefs her advice was to force the pre-teen to carry the child full term and deal with the situation as it played itself out.

Now, there are some areas that the clergy and religious counsel is well equipped to handle and bring about some wonderful healing and wholeness. But this was not one of those cases. My advice was for the mother to seek professional help and counsel for the child with those who are trained to medically, sociologically, and psychologically help and heal in that area.

Healing is of the utmost importance and the ultimate goal is to be able to finally get passed the hellish ordeals and events and bring some closure to these matters so that the true purpose of the person can be revealed and finally fulfilled.

If we are still carrying the hurts, wounds and pains from our tumultuous past, how can we enjoy living and be at peace with ourselves?

Hell is not only experienced after death for those who were bad and sinful on earth. No, my brothers and sisters, sometimes we live in our own types of hell, right here on earth. The hell of memories that constantly torment us with images of the past. The hell of fear that convinces us that we cannot and should not move on. The hell of hatred. Hatred of those who hurt us and most heinous... the hatred of ourselves.

We have got to know life in a better form than this. It's time to relieve ourselves of weights (things and people) that bring us down and carry on with the business of living. And I mean LIVING a real LIFE. What ever you have to do to do it... DO IT!!! Find a pastor that you can trust, or go to a competent doctor. Find help through psychological counseling or better yet, grab hold of God and pray until something happens. But by all means, let it all go and LIVE!!!!!

15

THE CONCLUSION OF THE MATTER

*A*t the beginning of my writing, I lent my family's history and our rather explicit ordeals to open up all of the subject matter for this book. I spoke of our major dysfunction, traumas, and tragedies in order to lay a foundation for the hope of healing that this book was intended to bring.

I laid bare a lot of private situations in my, and my family's lives that brought back many past memories, good and bad, that we had to deal with in some aspects all over again just to be a help to everyone who may happen to read this; and through our struggles and success, trust that the reader will find hope and help. But now, it's my greatest joy, pleasure, and privilege to bring you up to date with this, my wonderful family, and to finally bring closure to the entire matter.

To paraphrase the words of Joseph in Genesis, "The enemy meant it for our evil, but God meant it for our good!"

This family that went through living hell is now a healed family that is closer then we've ever been before. Now, you need to know that I almost got killed for some of the things that I exhumed from our family "burial ground". But the strange thing is that, in some manner, it served as a therapeutic vehicle to help us see that what we've endured and experienced has actually served to help others; and has caused us, as a family, to see and respect each other much more as adults looking back on some painful situations. But this time, we're looking at our past from the VICTORIOUS side! We've survived the assaults of seemingly hell, itself, and we ALL lived to remember, rejoice, laugh and tell about it. We're still standing!

My dad, whom I love with all of my heart, is a boot-legged preacher, now, working with me in the ministry. You all pray for me, so that he doesn't drive me crazy! Although he still wears a "deacon suit," he knows and teaches the Bible in a way that inspires others to think and search it out for themselves. He is totally delivered from alcohol, and has been for years.

It wasn't AA (although AA is a wonderful, and highly recommended organization for the readers struggling with alcohol as well as for their families) that brought him this deliverance; it was his faith in God. Man, you all should know my father! He's the clown's clown, and a barrel of laughs, yet, the voice of reason and sound advice. Even though he swears that his advice hasn't been taken, he needs to know that I'm living proof that it has. It truly has, Dad! How I love that man!

My mother, who is my heart through which I learned to love, is a great preacher who is also working with me in the ministry. When I can't make it to a service, I can call on her from time to time, and leave her to preach the gospel of our Lord Jesus Christ to the people. I know I'm talking like a proud father, but these are really the words from the heart of a very proud son.

She's a strong, WHOLE woman who has weathered every storm and come out MORE THAN A CONQUERER! Her addiction to prescription drugs lies far, far behind her, and she is intent on helping others through her past ordeals. And her love and pride for her children is still as "nauseatingly" strong as it was the day we were born. Maybe even stronger now. She's still the back-rubbing (all of my siblings are cringing right now), "Do you want me to make you something to eat?" or "I don't care how old you are, you're still my child!" lady that drives me crazy!!! At forty-something, I'm still her "Tooty-Looty!" How embarrassing! But, you gotta love her! I really can't imagine life without her. What a wonderful woman!!

All five of my sisters work with me in the ministry. And my nieces and nephews, too. All of my sisters are living for God, and raising the next generation in the same religious tradition that has kept us whole through these last four generations.

My only brother, Anthony, is the greatest artist that you'd ever want to see. His work is remarkable, and he has talent that is totally phenomenal. My talents are dwarfed by his abilities. Plus, he cuts a mean head of hair! He's happily married, living in Atlanta with his wife, Lorna. He beat me to it.

My grandmother, who is the matriarch of my family, is still as spry as a spring chicken. She's an octogenarian that carries the flame of life that I look forward to having at that age. Her mind and memory is as sharp as a tack, and she is as healthy as ever. She still switches when she walks. She's amazing. Still the most praying woman that I know, and loves God with every bit of her being. She's still good looking, too. Widowed, you know. So, any brother interested, just e-mail me and I'll hook you up. Boy, am I gonna get it.

> Yea, though I walk through the valley of the shadow of death, I will fear no evil: for thou art with me; thy rod and thy staff they comfort me. Psalm 23:4

When David wrote that, he didn't know that it would help me understand my family's troubles and triumphs. In order for us to walk into that valley, the Shepherd, Himself, had to lead us there. And if He led us into this valley, He would surely lead us out. He has done just that for us all.

As my pastor says: "If He leads you to it, He'll lead you through it!" We've been through the shadow of death, and we're STILL HERE! Why? Simple! Because He literally went with us! God honestly walked through this hell with us every step of the way, and led us all out with a living testimony of VICTORY! It took years to heal the wounds, but thank God, the wounds were healed. It took years to break some abusive patterns, but thank God, they're broken.

Eternal Victim? That's what the devil would love to make us think. But, he should have killed us when he had the chance. It's much too late, now. I know who I am, and I know the power that I possess! I am the head, and not the tail! I am above, and not beneath. Eternal Victim? You must be kidding! That was then, but never again! We ALL stand as ETERNAL VICTORS through Jesus Christ!

> *But thanks be to God, which giveth us the victory through our Lord Jesus Christ. 1 Cor. 15:57*

EPILOGUE

I want to leave you with these words of encouragement. I've said them before, and they have been a source of encouragement to many people. If you have heard me say these words, let them serve as a reminder. If not, never forget that if you do fall, you can get back up again and get back in your place.

The Bible says this:

For a just man falleth seven times, and riseth up again: but the wicked shall fall into mischief. Proverbs 24:16

Now what makes him just? We in the church would call him wicked if he falls seven times. One time we could understand–twice maybe–but seven times? What makes him just from the Bible's standpoint is that he has enough sense to realize that he can get back up. Not only can he get back up, he can get back in line.

No matter where you've fallen from, no matter what you've done, no matter how many times you've done it, it's not too late. He is so much in love with you that His mercy endures. His mercy is everlasting.

It's not too late. No matter what you've done, no matter where you've been, God is still faithful and He's still just. Even when we are unfaithful and when we're not just. He is so faithful and just, He'll forgive you of every single, solitary sin. No matter how many promises you've made and broken. No matter how many times you've done it over and over again.

I'm a living witness that He will forgive you like He forgave me. He's just waiting on you to confess. Just say, "Lord, have mercy. Forgive me. I'm not going to even make you any more promises. You know my heart. I want to do right. Show me how. Take me back. Put me back in line. I love You. Teach me how to walk right. Break every habit. Loose me from every addiction. Come into my life and my heart. Live in me and through me. I give you my life for the rest of my life."

Just that quickly, you're forgiven. Just that quickly, you're healed. He's your God and you're His child. There's no condemnation—no condemnation. Don't remember the past sins because God has forgotten them.

The prophet Isaiah reminds us:

I, even I, am he that blotteth out thy transgressions for mine own sake, and will not remember thy sins. Isaiah 43:25

If He's forgotten them then you forgive and forget too. You're healed; you're saved; you're whole, in Jesus' name.

ABOUT THE AUTHOR

Donnie McClurkin never intended to be one of the major gospel stories of the last decade. But with an abiding faith in the Lord, Donnie McClurkin begins the 21st century on the heels of a gold-selling album, with his dazzling Verity Record debut, *Live in London and More*.

His world was characterized by violence, alcoholism, and abuse, but young Donnie McClurkin found a safe haven in his church, Gospel Tabernacle Assemblies of God. It was there, at the age of nine, that he made a commitment to Christ. Throughout his troubled youth, amidst the strife of daily life, he learned to stand on the promises in these Scriptures:

> *A man's gift makes room for him, and brings him before great men. Prov 18:16*

> *I have set before thee an open door, and no man can shut it. Rev. 3:8.*

Donnie was born and raised in Amityville, New York. With a God-given gift for music that ran in his family, Donnie formed the McClurkin Singers with his siblings and several friends in 1979. It wasn't long before Donnie began to feel the first stirrings of a calling to preach as well as sing, as he does to this day. He went on to meet gospel legend Andrae Crouch who began a mentoring friendship that would shape the entire course of Donnie's future.

"I had listened to Andrae's music nearly all my life," says Donnie. "He had been a hero long before I ever met him. Entirely of his own initiative, he took me under his wing and became a teacher and role model to me. He was the influence in my life, spiritually and musically."

Donnie went on to form the New York Restoration Choir, which he recorded with in 1989. "The song *Speak to My Heart*, from *I Feel Well*, forged us a small but strong following in the gospel community," Donnie explains. "People started to know of the choir... each album after that had a big song on it that continued to build our reputation. God just got behind it, just like He got behind that rock David threw at Goliath!" He adds, chuckling, "It's all been nothing else but Him."

"Now who is going to tell me every bit of all that has happened to me is anything but the hand of God at work?!" asks Donnie. "It's got nothing to do with me! I'm just standing back amazed at what God's doing."

An appearance on the Oprah Winfrey Show, a few months later, and a recent song on the soundtrack to the hit animated film, *The Prince of Egypt* catapulted Donnie

McClurkin into the homes and consciousness of millions, creating the groundwell and setting the stage for the feverishly anticipated *Live in London and More*, now certified gold.

"I'm not going to take credit for what God has done... just give thanks," Donnie concludes. "Any successes I've had, any of the people He's put in my path... it's all been for His purposes. There are so many avenues through which we can serve Him. And wherever I am, as long as I know I'm in His purpose and plan, it will be right where He wants me to be."

Donnie McClurkin's message is clear, as real today as the day he committed his life to Christ at nine years old: "I want to introduce Jesus Christ to the world, not as a religious leader, but as an intimate friend who wants to radically change our lives," Donnie explains, "I want the world to know that we can sit down and embrace Him, He can embrace us, and He can handle any problem we are going through. He loves each of us individually, one by one."

Appendix

Resources for Rape Victims

The Rape, Abuse & Incest National Network (RAINN)
http://www.rainn.org
A non-profit organization based in Washington, D.C., operates a national hotline for survivors of sexual assault. The hotline 1-800.656.HOPE offers free, confidential counseling and support 24 hours a day, from anywhere in the country.

Resources for Domestic Violence

National Coalition Against Domestic Violence
http://www.ncadv.org
P.O. Box 18749
Denver, CO 80218
Phone: 303-839-1852
FAX: 303-831-9251

Family Violence Prevention Fund
383 Rhode Island Street, Suite 304
San Francisco, CA 94103-5133
Phone: 415-252-8900
FAX: 415-252-8991

National Coalition Against Domestic Violence
Policy Office
P.O. Box 34103
Washington, DC 20043-4103
Phone: 703-765-0339
FAX: 202-628-4899

National Battered Women's Law Project
275 7th Avenue, Suite 1206
New York, NY 10001
Phone: 212-741-9480
FAX: 212-741-6438

National Resource Center On DV
Pennsylvania Coalition Against Domestic Violence
6400 Flank Drive, Suite 1300
Harrisburg, PA 17112
Phone: 800-537-2238
FAX: 717-545-9456

Health Resource Center on Domestic Violence
Family Violence Prevention Fund
383 Rhode Island Street, Suite 304
San Francisco, CA 94103-5133
Phone: 800-313-1310
FAX: 415-252-8991

RESOURCES FOR CHILD MOLESTATION

Childhelp USA Child Abuse
Hotline: 800-4-A-CHILD (422-4453)
The Childhelp USA hotline is a national, twenty-four hour, toll-free hotline for child abuse. It's purpose is to take calls from anyone dealing with abuse and connect them with the agencies set up to report and deal with abuse in their state and locality.

RESOURCES FOR RUNAWAY CHILDREN AND TEENAGERS

National Runaway Switchboard
800-621-4000 (hotline), 312-880-9860 (business)
The National Runaway Switchboard is a toll-free crisis line operated by Chicago's Metro-Help. It operates twenty-four hours a day, year-long, and is designed to serve the needs of at-risk youth and their families. The phone lines are staffed by trained volunteers who use crisis intervention and active listening techniques to help callers identify their problems, explore options, and develop a plan of action. Their services are secular (non-religious), non-judgmental, and non-directive. Volunteers try to give callers factual information and confront irrational perceptions and solutions. They also offer message-relays (communication between runaways and parents without disclosing the location of the runaway) and referrals to over 8,000 social service agencies nationwide.

Runaway Hotline
800-231-6946 (hotline), 512-463-2000 (business)
P.O. Box 12428
Austin, TX 78711

The Runaway Hotline is a twenty-four hour, toll-free, nationwide hotline for children who have run away, are thinking about it, or have been thrown out of their homes. Like the National Runaway Switchboard, the Runaway Hotline serves as a nationwide information and referral center for runaways needing food, shelter, medical assistance, counseling, and related services. The goal of the hotline is to keep troubled youth safe and off the streets, so they can avoid becoming victims of crime and molestation, and to serve as a communication link between runaways and their families.

Covenant House
800-999-9999 "Nineline"
Covenant House, one of the largest privately funded child care agencies in the country, provides food, clothing, shelter, medical care, and counseling to 35,000 adolescents under the age of 21 each year. Founded in 1969 by a Catholic Priest, today Covenant House has shelters in New York, Toronto, Fort Lauderdale, Atlantic City, New Orleans, Houston, Los Angeles, Anchorage, and in three countries in Central America. The Nineline provides referrals and counseling for youth in need.

Children's Rights of America Youth Crisis Hotline
800-442-HOPE (4673), for crises.
800-874-111, for child abuses
The Children's Rights of America hotline offers support and crisis counseling for runaways and other youth. They make refferals to attornies in many areas, offer advocay for youth in abusive situations, and aid law enforcement and parents in locating youth.

National Center for Missing and Exploited Children
800-843-5678

National Youth Crisis Hotline (Christian Based)
800-448-4663
The National Youth Crises Hotline offers twenty-four hour crisis counseling, based upon the belief that Jesus Christ is the ultimate solution to teen runaways and problems facing teens in the world today. When a teen is on the street their objective is to get them immediately off of it, back to their parents or to the runaway shelter nearest them. They refer teens to a nationwide a list of shelters.

National Network of Runaway and Homeless Youth Services
202-783-7949
1319 F Street NW, Suite 201
Washington, DC 20004
The National Network's mission is to "challenge the nation and ourselves to provide positive alternatives to youth in high-risk situations and their families." Their programs include advocacy, public education, information dissemination, technical and training assistance, and an annual symposium. The Network represents over 900 agencies that serve youths and their families.

RESOURCES FOR ALCOHOL ADDITION

Alcoholics Victorious Christian 12 Step Support Groups
http://www.av.iugm.org
Find a local group in the Alcoholics Victorious International Directory. NOTE: With new groups formed all the time, this directory is being constantly updated.

CityTeam Ministries

http://www.cityteam.org/

CityTeam Ministries is in 12 cities and 8 countries. They have an outreach to the urban areas through recovery programs, rescue missions, youth outreach, and crisis pregnancy programs.

RESOURCES FOR DRUG ADDITION

Teen Challenge World Wide Network

Website: http://www.teenchallenge.com/

A comprehensive drug abuse awareness site, dedicated to helping those with life-controlling problems find the help they need.

RESOURCES FOR HOMOSEXUALS WHO WANT OUT

Exodus International

http://www.exodusnorthamerica.org

An international network of Christian ministries for those who want freedom from homosexuality through Jesus Christ.

Exodus Latinoamerica

http://www.newdirection.ca/exodusla/

Spanish-language materials for ministering to people trapped in homosexuality.

Desert Stream Ministries

http://www.desertstream.org/

A ministry to those who seek freedom from homosexuality and other sexual brokenness through Jesus Christ.

Journal of Human Sexuality

http://www.leaderu.com/menus/issues.html

A journal containing articles on homosexuality from a Christian perspective.

National Association for Research & Therapy of Homosexuality (N.A.R.T.H.)

http://www.narth.com
A national secular network of professional therapists who specialize in clinical reparative treatment for the homosexual.

One By One

http://www.oneby1.org
A site that addresses sexual woundedness within the Presbyterian Church USA.

PFOX - Parents & Friends of Ex-Gays

http://www.pfox.org/
A national network of Christian ministries for those who have friends and loved ones who are struggling with homosexuality.

Stonewall Revisited

http://www.stonewallrevisited.com/
A very comprehensive collection of articles and testimonies from ex-gays about the power of Jesus Christ to set people free from homosexuality.

Transforming Congregations

http://www.transformingcong.org/
A national network of churches (primarily United Methodist) who are committed to seeing the biblical standards of morality upheld while simultaneously offering hope and direction for those struggling with homosexuality.

AIDS Embracing Life Ministry
http://www.desertstream.org
A ministry to those suffering from AIDS and who seek help through Jesus Christ.

Christian Ministries for Homosexuality
http://www.messiah.edu/hpages/facstaff/chase/h/helplis.htm
A list of miscellaneous Christian organizations that specialize in homosexuality.

Homosexuality & Christianity Resource HomePage
http://www.messiah.edu/hpages/facstaff/chase/h/index.htm
This resource page is to provide education in the area of homosexuality and the Church as well as to provide resources for those who want to come out of the lifestyle through Jesus Christ.

Mastering Life Ministries
http://www.gospelcom.net/mlm/index.htm
Teaching and counseling resources for leaders and laity who struggle with or minister to sexually broken people, both heterosexual or homosexual.

RECOMMENDED BOOKS FOR HOMOSEXUALS WHO WANT OUT

Reparative Therapy of Male Homosexuality: A New Clinical Approach, by Dr Joseph Nicolosi / Jason Aronson Publisher

Origins and Treatment of Homosexuality: A Psychoanalytic Reinterpretation, by Dr Gerard Van Den Aardweg / Praeger Publisher

The Broken Image, by Leanne Payne / Crossway
Books Publisher

Counseling and Homosexuality, by Dr. Earl D. Wilson /
Word Publisher

Desires In Conflict, by Joe Dallas / Harvest House Publisher
(Homosexuality & Lesbianism)

Pursuing Sexual Wholeness, by Andrew Comiskey / Creation
House Publisher (Homosexuality & Lesbianism)

Out Of Egypt, by Jeanette Howard / Monarch Publisher
(Specifically Lesbianism and Emotional Dependency)

False Intimacy, by Dr. Harry W. Schaumburg /
Navpress Publisher

The Wounded Heart, by Dr. Dan Allendar /
Navpress Publisher

Coming Out of Homosexuality, by Bob Davies and Lori
Rentzel / Intervarsity Press Publishers

RESOURCES FOR SEXUAL ADDICTION

Esther Ministries
http://www.estheronline.org/main.htm
Esther Ministries is a non-profit organization established to
help women in relationship with sexually addicted men.

Stonegate Resources
http://www.stonegateresources.com/
The web site of Dr. Harry Schaumburg, author of one
of the best Christian books on sexual addiction,
False Intimacy.

EXXit - Escaping the Web of Temptation
http://www.exxit.org/
A site that helps people deal with sexual temptation–recommended by Focus on the Family.

Victims of Pornography

http://www.victimsofpornography.org/
Helping victims of pornography to be free from the nudity, sex and violence associated with pornography.

Pure Life Ministries

http://www.purelifeministries.org/
Dedicated to breaking the power of sexual addiction through the truth of God's Word and the power of the Cross of Jesus Christ by changing lives from the inside, helping hurting wives, and equipping church leaders.

Porn Prayer Support

http://www.jesus-connect.net/world/ppslinks/BattlePlan/
This site is quite extensive and covers every major area of sexual sin and brokenness.

Porn Free

www.Porn-Free.org
Help in breaking pornography addiction. This site is dedicated to sharing the good news that people can break free from pornography addiction. Sharing practical info on how to draw addiction-breaking power from a relationship with God, through Jesus Christ, empowered by God's Holy Spirit.

AUTHOR CONTACT

Donnie McClurkin
c/o Sierra Management
107 Hemlock Court
Hendersonville, TN 37075
1-615-822-5308
1-615-822-7527 (fax)
E-mail: sierramanagement@home.com

Visit Donnie's web site at:

www.DonnieMcClurkin.com